"Important and worth having. . . . First-person anecdotes from 'perfectionist' teens, cartoons and quizzes send the message in an informative, reassuring, and engaging way."
—*Youth Today*

Honored as a "Book for the Teen Age"
by the New York Public Library

Perfectionism

What's Bad About Being Too Good?

Miriam Adderholdt, Ph.D., and Jan Goldberg

Edited by Caryn Pernu

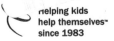

free spirit
PUBLiSHiNG

helping kids
help themselves™
since 1983

Library of Congress Cataloging-in-Publication Data

Adderholdt, Miriam, 1957–
    Perfectionism : what's bad about being too good? / Miriam Adderholdt and Jan Goldberg ; illustrated by Caroline Price Schwert.
    p. cm.
    Originally published: Minneapolis, MN : Free Spirit Pub., c1987.
    Includes bibliographical references and index.
    Summary: Discusses the dangers of being a perfectionist, with tips for easing up on oneself, gaining control over life, and getting professional help.
    ISBN 1-57542-062-7
    1. Perfectionism (Personality trait) Juvenile literature.
2. Mental health Juvenile literature. [1. Perfectionism (Personality trait)] I. Goldberg, Jan. II. Price, Caroline, ill. III. Title.
BF698.35.P47A23   1999
158.1—dc21

99-23088
CIP

At the time of this book's publication, all facts and figures cited are the most current available. All telephone numbers, addresses, and Web site URLs are accurate and active; all publications, organizations, Web sites, and other resources exist as described in this book; and all have been verified as of February 2005. The authors and Free Spirit Publishing make no warranty or guarantee concerning the information and materials given out by organizations or content found at Web sites, and we are not responsible for any changes that occur after this book's publication. If you find an error or believe that a resource listed here is not as described, please contact Free Spirit Publishing. Parents, teachers, and other adults: We strongly urge you to monitor children's use of the Internet.

Cover design by Circus Design
Cover illustration and book design by Marieka Heinlen
Illustrations by Caroline Price Schwert
Index prepared by Kay Schlembach

15 14 13 12 11 10 9 8
Printed in the United States of America

Free Spirit Publishing Inc.
217 Fifth Avenue North, Suite 200
Minneapolis, MN 55401-1299
(612) 338-2068
help4kids@freespirit.com
www.freespirit.com

Free Spirit Publishing is a member of the Green Press Initiative, and we're committed to printing our books on recycled paper containing a minimum of 30% post-consumer waste (PCW). For every ton of books printed on 30% PCW recycled paper, we save 5.1 trees, 2,100 gallons of water, 114 gallons of oil, 18 pounds of air pollution, 1,230 kilowatt hours of energy, and .9 cubic yards of landfill space. At Free Spirit it's our goal to nurture not only young people, but nature too!

green press INITIATIVE

Dedication

To the memory of my father, the Rev. C.C. Adderholdt.
His love of learning and quest for knowledge
were instilled within me at an early age.
M.A.

To the memory of my beloved parents, Sam and Sylvia Lefkovitz.
Because of them, my world was always filled with books.
J.G.

Acknowledgments

I want to thank Dr. Mary Frasier of the University of Georgia for her immense help while directing my doctoral dissertation. Her expertise in the fields of gifted education, counseling, and bibliotherapy were invaluable to both my dissertation and this book. Her kindness, concern, and long hours were greatly appreciated.

Thanks to Tom Greenspon, Ph.D., whose comments and direction have been invaluable in shaping both the first edition and this revision.

Thanks to my publisher, Judy Galbraith, whose first and foremost concern is the welfare of gifted children. She is extremely talented and we in gifted education benefit from her dedication.

Thanks also to my family for their continued support in my life and career. I'm ever grateful to my mother, Mrs. C.C. Adderholdt, and my brother, Mark P. Adderholdt.

—Miriam Adderholdt

I want to thank Judy Galbraith for the wonderful opportunity to work with Free Spirit. Many thanks to my editor, Caryn Pernu, for the chance to work on this interesting project. Her team approach, helpful manner, cheerful disposition, and important insights were much appreciated.

Heartfelt thanks to my family for their ongoing love and support. A very special thank you to daughters Sherri and Debbie, son-in-law Bruce, and incredible husband, Larry. I couldn't do it without you!

—Jan Goldberg

Contents

How Much of a Perfectionist Are You?

> Have no fear of perfection—you'll never reach it.
>
> —Salvador Dali

Have you ever caught yourself thinking or feeling something like this?

- "My family expects me to win, and I can't let them down."
- "I started it, so I have to finish it."
- "If I don't do that, everyone will be so disappointed."
- "I want everyone to like me."
- "I have to do everything well, not just the things I know I'm good at."
- "They are just saying I did well to be nice."
- "Can't they see I'm a fraud?"
- "It would have been perfect if I could have done it by myself."

If any of these sound familiar to you, there's a good chance you have perfectionist tendencies.

How much of a perfectionist are you? The quiz on the next page can help you find out.

Quick Quiz !

Read each statement; then rate each one according to the following scale:

Strongly agree +2
Agree somewhat +1
Can't decide 0
Disagree somewhat -1
Strongly disagree -2

Answer with your *first* thought to get the truest response.

1. I'm critical of people who don't live up to my expectations.

2. I get upset if I don't finish something I start.

3. I do things precisely down to the very last detail.

4. I argue about test scores I don't agree with, even when they won't affect my final grade.

5. After I finish something, I often feel dissatisfied.

6. I feel guilty when I don't achieve something I set out to do.

7. When a teacher hands back one of my papers, I look immediately for my mistakes, not at what I did well.

8. I compare my test scores with those of other good students in my class.

9. It's hard for me to laugh at my own mistakes.

10. If I don't like the way I've done something, I start over and keep at it until I get it right.

Now add up your ratings to learn where you fall on the Perfectionism Continuum.

---

1. Adapted from "Some People Are Perfect . . . Or Try to Be!" *Current Health* Vol. 2, January 1978 (17–19). Permission granted by the publisher, General Learning Corporation.

+15 to +20   **Too Good to Be True.** Maybe you're exaggerating because people have always expected you to be perfect.

+10 to +14   **Too Good for Your Own Good.** You're trying too hard—and it's time to ask yourself why.

+5 to +9   **Borderline Perfectionist.** Certain events may push you over the line into full-fledged perfectionism, but you usually roll with the punches without going to extremes.

+1 to +4   **Healthy Pursuer of Excellence.** You enjoy doing well, but you can turn your pursuit of excellence on and off (in other words, *you* drive *it*, not the other way around). You probably spread your talents and abilities into several areas: academics, friendships, your health and appearance, hobbies, and play.

0 to -5   **You're Used to Hanging Loose.** Maybe you've made a conscious effort to be less perfectionistic, or maybe you were born knowing how to relax and take it easy.

-6 to -10   **A Little TOO Relaxed.** Your favorite song is "Que Sera, Sera" ("What Will Be, Will Be") and your favorite activity is lying in a hammock feeling the earth turn. A slight exaggeration, perhaps, but there is such a thing as overdoing underdoing.

-11 to -20   **Barely Breathing.** And maybe you're exaggerating your own coolness. Read through the statements again, and this time respond to them honestly. You can't be apathetic about everything!

Did this exercise teach you something you didn't already know? Probably not; most perfectionists are aware of who and what they are. But one thing you may not know is that you're not alone. Dr. David Burns of Stanford University estimates that about half the population of the United States has perfectionist tendencies. These tendencies in moderation aren't bad. Wanting to achieve and persistently trying to succeed are signs of the healthy pursuit of excellence. But when *what* you achieve becomes *who* you are, when you tie yourself in knots trying to meet your own high expectations or to please your parents and teachers and coaches and friends, that's a problem. When you're too afraid to take healthy risks, that's a problem.

Perfectionist tendencies seem to exist on a continuum—ranging from healthy to dysfunctional behaviors. But there's a big difference between the healthy pursuit of excellence and the unhealthy striving for an impossible ideal. People who strive for excellence may have a strong need for order and organization and high expectations for themselves, but they also accept their own mistakes and have positive ways of coping. They admire role models who emphasize doing one's best, and they enjoy their parents' high expectations of them.

Perfectionists, on the other hand, live in a constant state of anxiety about making errors. They have extremely high standards and perceive excessive expectations and negative criticisms from others, including their parents. Sometimes those external pressures are real, sometimes they come from within. Perfectionists question their own judgments, lack effective coping strategies, and feel a constant need for approval. They fear being exposed as frauds or imposters. Many avoid the healthy risks that will help them grow, procrastinating or refusing outright to try new experiences for fear of failure.

Gifted kids in particular can struggle with perfectionism. In *The Gifted Kids' Survival Guide (A Teen Handbook),* authors Judy Galbraith and Jim Delisle report that "forty-six percent of our survey respondents wanted help learning how to give themselves permission to fail sometimes—to be more gentle with themselves and not set their own expectations so high."

Why are gifted kids especially prone to perfectionism, and why is it a particular gripe for them? Many have a long history of A's and A+'s in school, and they've come to expect academic perfection. They often carry this desire for perfection into other areas of their lives. Many are so used to success that when they do less than the best, they feel like failures. It hurts so much that they decide never to let it happen again.

What's bad about being too good? For some people, plenty. The need to be the best can drive some people to extremes.

On January 6, 1994, United States national champion figure skater Nancy Kerrigan was attacked in Detroit as she left the rink after a practice session at the U.S. Olympic trials. A favorite to win a gold medal at the 1994 Winter Olympics, Kerrigan suffered a knee injury from a blow wielded by an assailant. Her elimination from the competition spelled good news to another skater, Tonya Harding, also in contention for the number one spot.

Eventually accused of hiring someone to attack Kerrigan, Harding admitted to knowing of the plot after the assault. Harding's husband and her bodyguard were convicted in the incident. Though implicated in the attack, Harding went on to compete in the Olympics and to win the 1994 U.S. National Ladies' Figure Skating competition. She was later stripped of her title and banned from competitive skating for life.

Harding paid dearly for this incident—losing her career and her marriage. What drove her to it? Possibly the drive to be the best—even if it means trying to win at any cost.

You probably haven't ever thought of going to extremes to eliminate your competition—most perfectionists don't—but maybe you have felt like screaming over the pressure you feel from inside and outside. Does closing the door to your room and staying there forever, or telling your parents and teachers and friends *just leave me alone!* sound attractive? Perfectionism can be a heavy burden because, let's face it, nobody's perfect.

This book is not about pursuing excellence; there's nothing wrong with that. Rather, it's about the impossibility of perfection. It's about learning to strike a balance between the three main areas of life: (1) work and school, (2) play and hobbies, and (3) family and social relationships. It shows you why it's important to give yourself a break every now and then, to be pleased with who and what you are, here and now, and to enjoy the healthy pursuit of excellence.

What's the difference between perfectionism and the pursuit of excellence?

The Pursuit of Excellence	Perfectionism
Doing the research necessary for a term paper, working hard on it, turning it in on time, and feeling good about what you learned.	Doing three drafts, staying up two nights in a row, and handing your paper in late because you had to get it right (and still feeling bad about your paper).
Studying for a test, taking it with confidence, and feeling good about your score of 96.	Cramming at the last minute, taking the test with sweaty palms, and feeling bad about your 96 because a friend got a 98.
Choosing to work on group projects because you enjoy learning from the varied experiences and approaches of different people.	Always working alone because no one can do as good a job as you—and you're not about to let anyone else slide by on your A.
Accepting an award with pride even though the engraver misspelled your name. (You know it can be fixed later.)	Accepting the award resentfully because those idiots didn't get your name right.
Reading the story you wrote for the school paper and noticing that the editor improved the copy.	Throwing a fit because the editor tampered with your work.
Going out with people who are interesting, likable, and fun to be with.	Refusing to go out with people who aren't stellar athletes, smart, and popular.
Being willing to try new things, take risks, and learn from your experiences and your mistakes.	Avoiding new experiences because you are terrified of making mistakes—especially in public.
Deciding to baby-sit to earn some extra money, taking a baby-sitting class through the local park district.	Deciding to organize and run a baby-sitting service for all of the families from the local elementary school.
Keeping your room cleaner and neater, making your bed more often and putting your clothes away.	Not being able to leave the room until the bed and room are just so.
Taking tennis lessons and playing two or three times a week to have fun and joining a competitive league to challenge yourself.	Taking lessons as often as you can, practicing every day, and not feeling satisfied until you can beat every other player in your league.

Some people devote their lives to the misguided pursuit of perfection. Like Adam, who used to drop courses rather than risk getting a B—and then have to go to summer school to make up the courses he dropped. And Jen, who stuffed her locker with term papers she refused to turn in because "they weren't good enough"—and ended up getting C's for not handing in her work.

This book comes out of experience, studies, and the proof we've seen that you can put the lid on perfectionism. And you don't have to sacrifice any of your will to succeed, your push to achieve, or your desire to be the best you can be.

Hard to believe? Then read what three reformed perfectionists have to say:

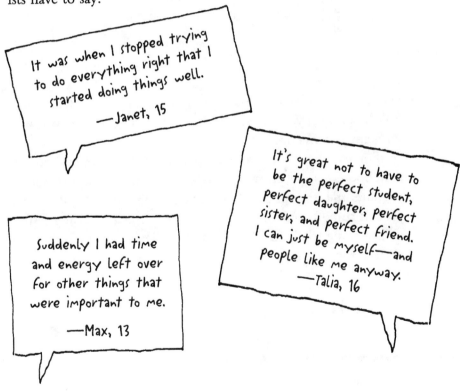

It was when I stopped trying to do everything right that I started doing things well.
—Janet, 15

It's great not to have to be the perfect student, perfect daughter, perfect sister, and perfect friend. I can just be myself—and people like me anyway.
—Talia, 16

Suddenly I had time and energy left over for other things that were important to me.
—Max, 13

Conquering your perfectionism may release other abilities you didn't know you had. And it will certainly make your life easier, more relaxed, more satisfying—and a lot more fun.

1

Why People Become Perfectionists

> The essence of being human is that one does not seek perfection.
>
> —George Orwell

Perfectionism isn't a disease; you didn't catch it. Perfectionism isn't hereditary; you weren't born with it. So how did you end up being a perfectionist?

Some experts believe that perfectionism develops during childhood. Family pressure, self-pressure, social pressure, media pressure, and unrealistic role models combine in a Big Push that propels some people into a lifetime of worrying, feeling guilty, and working too hard. They come to believe that unless they are perfect, they are unworthy of love and respect.

Does Birth Order Matter?

According to Kevin Leman, Ph.D., author of *The New Birth Order Book*, firstborn children may have a greater propensity for perfectionism. Families often reward "eager beaver" behavior, especially in a firstborn child. There may be several reasons for this. For one, first-time parents can be insecure. If their young son or daughter turns out to be a real go-getter, they're likely to think, "Hey, we're doing a great job as parents!" And they go on to encourage and reinforce fast-track learning.

Firstborn children also tend to spend more time around adults than do children who come later. They learn adult vocabulary, model adult behaviors, and measure themselves according to adult standards of achievement. And adults may reinforce this by expecting them to live up to those standards. Not surprisingly, firstborns are identified as gifted and talented more often than any-other-borns. They tend to be great organizers and may be very achievement-oriented. But

they're also more likely to get counseling. And they are more likely to cross the line from pursuing excellence to striving for perfection.

Being a firstborn doesn't mean you'll be a perfectionist, however, and being born somewhere else in the order doesn't mean you won't. The relationship isn't that simple. There are plenty of second- and thirdborn perfectionists, and many first-borns content to slide amiably through life. That's because there are numerous other reasons why some kids develop perfection-ist traits—such as growing up with perfectionist parents or inter-nalizing the messages of other important influences.

The Push to Achieve

All parents want their children to be smart and successful, but some parents push too hard. In their desire to be the "perfect" parents, they propel their children to be the "perfect" sons or daughters. They inadvertently give their children the message "Our love and affection depend on your ability to do well."

And this message can start very young. With the growing body of research on the brain development in the crucial first years, many perfectionist parents strive to give their children a boost as early as possible. They begin reading and talking to their child long before he or she is born. Then, when the baby does come into the world, the parents keep up their efforts to make sure that their son or daughter gets ahead and stays there.

High expectations from parents and early stimulation can be very good for children. Over the last three decades, many studies have shown that high-quality preschool can boost later achievement and social adjustment, reduce the likelihood of placement in special education, and increase the chances of graduation from high school. But some parents push these findings a bit too far and develop expectations that are far too high.

One way they do this is by piling on activity after activity: baby gymnastics and swimming, music lessons for tots, French for toddlers, and so on. Some even advocate teaching babies as young as three months to read.

Just as florists get flowering plants to bloom early by raising them in a greenhouse and carefully controlling light and temperature, some parents try to give their children's development a

head start by providing them with extra stimulation and opportunities for learning skills ahead of other children the same age. This approach generates controversy. On one side are those who feel that kids can and should learn more and sooner; on the other are those who believe childhood is already too short. The more time a child spends on structured activities, the less time available for the free play that gives rise to creative thinking, they argue.

As kids hit school age, many continue to be super-scheduled by their parents—piano lessons, ballet classes, enrichment tutoring, soccer, softball, ice-skating, swimming, scouts, art and music camps, organized play groups, and on and on and on. In moderation, these are all excellent activities. But together they can result in circuit overload.

Many authorities in childhood education speak out against pushing children too hard, too soon:

Pediatrician Benjamin Spock voiced strong objections to fast-track schooling and forcing kids into the fast lane. He believed that our society is much too concerned with competition and materialism and instead should focus on other values—like cooperation and kindness.

Dr. Sylvia Rimm, a child psychologist, emphasizes that parents must set realistic goals for achievement and provide children with balanced activities.

Fred Rogers, known to several generations as Mr. Rogers, is the star of the longest-running children's program on public TV, *Mr. Rogers' Neighborhood*. In his mild, reassuring style, Rogers always stresses that all individuals are important, unique, and special "just the way they are" and that qualities like friendship, compassion, and goodness are of the utmost importance.

More and more, experts are questioning whether children who start school knowing more than their peers actually stay ahead in the years to come. Many psychologists say that instead of pressuring little kids to learn facts and read flash cards, it's better to take them on nature walks, build sand castles with them, and spend time together playing imaginative games and enjoying unstructured activities.

In other words, pushing kids too hard to achieve very early may not lead to lasting effects. And the price may not be worth it. Too much stress may even block learning.

The Workaholic Kid

We've heard of workaholic adults—but workaholic kids? According to psychologist Erik Erikson, children between ages six and twelve are at risk for becoming workaholics if they are rewarded only for the things they do rather than for the personal qualities they have and are developing. In other words, children who are praised for bringing home perfect papers but not for being friendly, having a sense of humor, being playful, taking risks, or showing kindness and gentleness are likely to think that work is the most important part of life. These children get hooked on working hard because they know it will bring rewards.

Work can be as psychologically addictive as drugs or gambling. Unlike drugs or gambling, however, it's something that parents, teachers, and coaches support and encourage without realizing the danger. The father who brags that Alvin spends four hours a day on his homework probably isn't aware that Alvin may be better off spending some of that time just having fun. But if the family keeps rewarding Alvin for sitting at his desk, that's what he'll keep doing.

Studies have shown that workaholics suffer from higher stress levels and have a greater tendency to burn out than people whose lives are more balanced. Some workaholics literally don't know how to relax; they work day in and day out without ever taking a vacation. It's hardly a healthy lifestyle.

It's important to work, but it's also important to play. It's good to study, but it's good to goof off on occasion. Straight A's are commendable, but so is an active social life.

In order that people may be happy in their work, these three things are needed: They must be fit for it. They must not do too much of it. And they must have a sense of success in it.

—John Ruskin

Think about your life. Where do you spend your time? How much time each week do you spend . . .

- Doing creative activities such as music, theater, painting, writing, photography, knitting, or other arts?

- Participating in sports, clubs, or organizations at school or in your community?

- Talking with family members or doing other family activities?

- Doing service or volunteer work in your school or community?

- Participating in a religious or spiritual community?

- Watching television, surfing the Net, or playing computer games?

- Doing chores?

- Working?

- Studying or doing homework?

- Reading for pleasure?

- Enjoying your friends?

- Sleeping?

- Eating healthy, regular meals?

How balanced is your life? Are there some important areas you're neglecting? Are there areas where you're spending too much time? What would you change if you could? (And how soon can you start?)

Media Messages

The next time you watch TV, pay attention to how many times *perfect* is used as part of a sales pitch. You'll see ads for "perfect" cars, ice cream, soap, vacations, jeans, nail polish, dog food—you name it. But cars break down, some soaps make us itch, vacations can be plagued by sunburn and mosquitoes . . . you get the idea. Regardless of what copywriters claim, nothing is perfect!

Now consider how *perfect* is used to describe how we should live and the relationships we should strive for. We've all heard of the "perfect romance," the "perfect marriage," and the "perfect family." But romances fizzle, many marriages end in divorce, and the typical family has occasional arguments and off days.

TV, magazines, and the movies lead us to believe that everyone should be thin, gorgeous, rich, and successful. Moms, dads, and other caregivers should have all the answers, work all day and come home to fix a special dinner for their families, take care of the house, entertain friends, and help the kids with their homework. We see television families living in perfectly decorated luxury, wearing the hottest fashions, driving pricey cars, and never having to take out the trash. We're told that it's possible to have perfect homes and perfect jobs, perfect complexions, and perfect bodies. We know that's not how things really are, but we wish they could be that way—and we sometimes convince ourselves that we can make them that way if we try hard enough.

It's a challenge to resist the pressures to be perfect that we get from our families, our culture, and the media. It's difficult not to compound these by setting unrealistic goals and pushing ourselves to achieve more and faster and younger. It's tough to let go of the belief that we can do anything we set out to do. After all, we're bright, capable, energetic—what's to stop us?

There's nothing wrong with wanting to do our best; there's nothing wrong with setting goals and achieving them, but taking those healthy desires and pushing them to the extreme is different. It's perfectionism. It messes with our minds, and it messes up our bodies.

Check It Out!

All Grown Up and No Place to Go: Teenagers in Crisis by David Elkind, Ph.D. (Reading, MA: Addison Wesley Longman Inc., 1997). Talks about how teenagers are pressured into growing up quickly and discusses some of the problems that result.

The Beauty Trap by Elaine Landau (New York: New Discovery Books, 1994). Combines recent studies with personal interviews to examine the effects of the beauty myth—the unrealistic expectations teenage girls adopt when they buy in to the beauty and fashion industries' portrayal of perfection as an attainable and pursuable goal.

The New Birth Order Book by Kevin Leman, Ph.D. (Grand Rapids, MI: Baker Book House, 1998). Many teens find that this adult book offers a fascinating, in-depth discussion of how birth order affects who you are and what you do in all areas of your life.

Real Gorgeous: The Truth About Body & Beauty by Kaz Cooke (New York: W.W. Norton & Company, 1996). An empowering book that tells girls and women how to be friends with their bodies. It's packed with jokes, cartoons, and practical ways to find real self-esteem and avoid freak-outs and rip-offs.

Birth Order Home Page
www.birthorderplus.com
Includes a number of links to a variety of birth order topics: Birth Order Characteristics, Birth Order Comparisons, Birth Order Test: What Is Your Birth Order?

2

What Perfectionism Does to Your Mind

> The pursuit of excellence is gratifying and healthy.
> The pursuit of perfection is frustrating, neurotic,
> and a terrible waste of time.
>
> —Edwin Bliss

When a group of University of Georgia women students were tested to determine the relationship between perfectionism and self-concept, a fascinating pattern emerged: The higher their perfectionism score, the lower their self-concept score. The young women were tying their identities to their performance.

You've heard people say things like, "There's Kai. She's a straight-A student." The trouble is, Kai has heard it, too, and that's how she defines herself. What happens if she gets a B? Her sense of herself might feel shaken. She feels that she's just not "herself." It doesn't matter that she still looks the same, has the same values, likes the same foods, and wears the same battered sneakers; she feels different.

The Perfectionist Thinking of
5 Famous People

Leonardo da Vinci—artist and engineer
"I have offended God and mankind because my work didn't reach the quality it should have."

Katharine Hepburn—actor
"I think most of the people involved in any art always secretly wonder whether they are really there because they're good—or because they're lucky."

Abraham Lincoln—U.S. president
The Gettysburg Address was "a flat failure."

Marie Curie—chemist
"I never see what has been done; I only see what remains to be done."

Sor Juana Inés de la Cruz—poet
This brilliant seventeenth century writer cut off her hair "in punishment for my head's ignorance" for not learning Latin fast enough.

If you think about it, tying your identity to having a straight-A average is a poor choice. It's simply too hard to maintain. (One B and it's all over!) A number of straight-A high school students, determined to keep it up once they hit college, try to ignore the fact that the competition has suddenly gotten much tougher. High schools have to let everybody in, but colleges get to choose their students among thousands of applicants.

One young man found out what this meant during the first assembly at his college. He'd been a star performer all during high school—straight A's, National Merit Scholarship finalist, near-perfect SAT scores, and valedictorian. He learned that day

that nearly half the members of his freshman class had been vale-
dictorians, too. Suddenly he was a small fish in a big pond.

People who pursue excellence enjoy their achievements and
take pride in their accomplishments, but they don't depend on
them for their entire self-worth. Perfectionists tend to link their
identities with their achievements: winning trophies and awards,
setting records, getting the lead in the school play, being elected
student-body president—even being identified as gifted.

A perfectionist whose identity is at stake may go to desperate lengths to try to save it. Some students lose sleep and make
themselves sick trying to maintain their winning selves. Some
cheat. Some tune out and drop out rather than face what they
perceive as "failure." Some turn to alcohol or drugs.

Games Perfectionists Play

When you start believing that achievement and self-worth are
one and the same, your thinking becomes convoluted.
Perfectionists use a number of tricks and stratagems—often
unconsciously—to protect the picture they have of themselves.
Do any of these sound familiar?

Riding the Mood Roller Coaster. You set a goal for yourself (for example: to ace a math test). You do it—and you feel great!

But you don't ace the next one—you get an 89. And you feel *awful*. Your friends and family notice and try to reassure you, but you're prickly and irritable and suspicious of their motives. Why would they praise you? You're not worth it; you couldn't even get that A you were after!

Then along comes the next math test, you ace it, and you're riding high again. It's exhausting! You feel excited and capable when you do well, and unacceptable and ashamed when you don't.

The Numbers Game. The quantity of achievements or actions becomes more important than the quality. You start to focus on how many trophies you win, papers you write, awards you receive, honors you reap—not what you're learning or what they're really worth. No number is ever high enough; you just keep counting.

Focusing on the Future. You give an especially brilliant speech during the debate. Everybody comes up afterward and tells you that you were inspiring. But all you can think about is what you forgot to say. Or your mind is already on next week's essay contest—what if you don't outdo yourself in that, too?

Don't even try to sit back and savor your success; that's not what perfectionists do. There's no time—not when you're already planning the future and worrying about the things you must do to succeed.

Pining over the Past. "If only I'd . . ." "Why didn't I . . ." "This wouldn't have happened if I'd started sooner . . ." "If I'd put down that answer, I would've got an A instead of a B." You don't let things go. You chew on them relentlessly, like a dog gnawing on a bone. Thoughts like these keep you stuck in the same old groove of the same old record.

Telescopic Thinking. You use both ends of a telescope when viewing your achievements. When looking at the goals you haven't met, you use the magnifying end so they appear much larger than they really are. But when looking at those you have met, you use the "minifying" end so they appear minute and insignificant.

For example, you win the district tennis match, but you can't feel good about it because you haven't won the state. Or you compete in the state tournament, making it all the way to the championship match, but feel outclassed the minute your opponent pulls ahead.

Putting Your Goals First. Given a choice between sleeping and studying, you study—even if it means drinking gallons of coffee or taking caffeine pills, pinching yourself to stay awake, and making yourself sick. Or given the choice between going out with friends or working on your volleyball serve, you opt for the gym. Your achievement goals always come before fun or friends or your own good health.

Getting It Right. You're not satisfied with anything but the best, most perfect results, so you do the same thing again . . . and again . . . and again until you get it right. Maybe you repeat the same course in school until you get the A you're determined to have. Or you play the same piece of music over and over and over and over and over and over and over and over and over and over again, hating yourself because you're so slow. You're worried that others will know how hard you worked when you want it to appear effortless.

All-or-Nothing Thinking. You're not satisfied unless you have it all—all the track trophies, all the academic awards your school can give, all the leadership positions in your clubs. One B or one second place is enough to tip you over into the feeling that you've failed, that you're not good enough.

Sometimes parents encourage this attitude. When Lisa started seventh grade, her parents said, "We'll give you ten dollars for each A on your report card—as long as you get all A's. If you get one B, we won't give you anything." Lisa learned something besides all-or-nothing thinking. She learned that her parents' love and approval depended on her performance.

A Perfectionist Myth

The Fall of Icarus

When master craftsman Daedalus and his son, Icarus, were imprisoned in a labyrinth by King Minos of Crete, Daedalus worked hard to plan their escape. For years he collected the feathers that fell from the birds who flew over the labyrinth. Then he fashioned frames from wood and attached the feathers to the frames with wax and twine. He made a pair of wings for himself, and another for his son. As he was helping Icarus strap on his wings, Daedalus warned him to keep a middle course over the sea—not to fly too close to the heat of the sun or too near to the dampness of the sea.

When the two sailed out into the air, over the sea toward freedom, Icarus had never felt such exhilaration. His great wings carried him effortlessly over the waves. Filled with a sense of power, he flew higher and higher still, the better to look down on the rest of the world. Why not go five feet more, then ten feet, then twenty?

Daedalus shouted to him, but Icarus ignored his father. Then it happened: The wax melted, Icarus's wings came apart, and he fell like a stone into the sea.

The Procrastination Trap

How could a perfectionist also be a procrastinator? At first blush, it might be difficult to believe, but it's quite common. Studies have shown that in many cases, perfectionism is at the core of procrastination.

For the perfectionist, procrastination acts as an insurance policy. Perfectionists must get everything right, so any performance short of spectacular is a "failure." Naturally this piles on the pressure. To delay the possibility that a performance might not be perfect, the perfectionist puts things off.

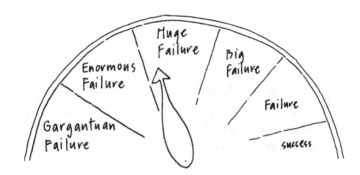

And then the inevitable happens: The panic buzzer sounds! The test is tomorrow morning, or the paper is due Monday and it's already Saturday night. Now the perfectionist goes into overdrive, pulling all-nighters and working furiously to get the job done. Needless to say, quality suffers. But in the perfectionist's mind, that's okay—because how can you possibly do a perfect job if you simply don't have enough time?

For some perfectionists, starting a new project is almost a turnoff because each new beginning is a step on the road to possible failure.

Sue was in her first year of college when her procrastination habit caught up with her. As usual, she waited until the last minute before studying for a final. Knowing she'd be up all night, she decided to go to the classroom to study so she wouldn't keep her roommate awake. She attended a small private school for women, so she simply threw on a coat over her nightgown and headed out. She got to the classroom, studied most of the night, and just before dawn, decided to take a short nap. She thought she'd sleep only a few minutes.

Several hours later, she awoke to find the class staring down at her!

This incident has its funny side, but others aren't funny at all. Some perfectionists lose a shot at admission to college because they didn't get their applications in on time. Others lose their jobs because they can't let go of one project and move on to the next. Or they get so far behind in their schoolwork that they finally give up and drop out.

Procrastination is a complex problem that leads to irrational behavior. Perfectionists often resort to one (or more) of the following to help hide their fear of being "imperfect":

■ **Not starting a project.** "If I don't start something," perfectionists think, "I can't fail." So they write letters, watch TV, surf the Net, clean out their desk—anything to keep busy and avoid the work that really needs doing.

■ **Not handing in a finished project.** "It's kind of done," perfectionists think, "but it's not good enough!" Often, procrastinating students ask for an incomplete grade rather than risk getting less than an A. There's always just a little bit more that needs to be added or tweaked.

- **Starting so many projects** that there isn't time to complete any one of them. "If only I didn't have so much to do," perfectionists think, "I'd do a great job!" Projects, assignments, and papers pile up until there's no way to finish any of them, much less all of them. Taking on too much is a common way of procrastinating.

Joseph R. Ferrari, Ph.D., associate professor of psychology at DePaul University, explains, "The term *procrastination* comes directly from the Latin verb *procrastinare,* which means quite literally, 'to put off or postpone until another day.'" Ferrari, coauthor of *Procrastination and Task Avoidance—Theory, Research, and Treatment* (New York: Plenum Publishing, 1995), is also a member of the Procrastination Research Group at Carleton University.

According to Ferrari, some people put way too much time on one aspect of a project while allowing little or no time for the rest. They can then blame any failure or incompleteness on lack of sufficient time. "And they can also rationalize that any failure was not due to lack of effort, since they spent so much time trying," says Ferrari.

All of this may be tied to something else: self-protection. Many perfectionists procrastinate out of a desire to be liked by others. Wanting to please the important people in their lives and protect their self-esteem, perfectionists often feel anxiety over what others think about their performance. And that anxiety may lead to procrastination.

If you're caught in the procrastination trap, here are ten "escape tips" for you to try. You don't have to try them all. Just pick a tip that seems right for you. Choose one and get going—don't put it off!

He who hesitates is last.

—Mae West

10 Tips for Procrastinators

1. Allow more time than you think a project will take. For example, if you think writing an essay will take two hours, plan three or even four hours to do it.

2. Set realistic goals, but don't set them in stone. Stay flexible.

3. Break down big and intimidating projects into smaller, more manageable steps.

4. Start something right now—instead of waiting until you feel thoroughly prepared.

5. Make a conscious effort to realize that your paper, project, or whatever can't be perfect. Getting a grasp on this fact helps deflate the fear of failure.

6. Begin your day with your most difficult task or the one you enjoy least. The rest of the day will seem easy by comparison.

7. Plan to have fun without feeling guilty. Start with the things you most enjoy doing—the things you usually save for last and don't get around to at all. Then add the things you're supposed to do.

8. Keep a diary of your progress. List the things you accomplish each day. Read it over from time to time and feel proud of what you've done. Reward yourself.

9. Remove distractions from your workspace. Keep food, TV, magazines, games, the Internet, and other temptations out of your way. Don't go to the library and get lost in a book on ancient Egypt when you're looking for information on civil rights.

10. Keep a list of backup projects—things you mean to do when you have time. Once you've tackled your procrastination, you'll have the time to do them. Use it productively!

Writer's Block, Test Anxiety, and Other Problems for Perfectionists

Can't put pen to paper? Too timid to touch the keyboard? Maybe you're afraid that what you're about to write won't be up to your own too-high standards. Writer's block is a common complaint for perfectionists.

Sweaty palms and a speedy heartbeat on the morning of the test? No wonder you're anxious; there's a chance you might not get a perfect score.

Has your get-up-and-go got up and went? Even the most hardworking student can become frustrated after years of attempting the impossible. The result, oddly enough, is laziness. Questions like "What's the use?" and "Why should I even try?" start making sense. The dynamics behind this phenomenon are more complex than simple sloth, but the end result is the same: The perfectionist lies around and does little or nothing.

Do you suffer frequent bouts with the blues? Times when it doesn't seem worth it to climb out of bed? Headaches, listlessness, crying jags? These are all signs of depression, one of the many ways perfectionism can affect your mind.

WARNING!!!

IF YOU ARE FEELING DEPRESSED, TELL SOMEONE TODAY.

Start with your parents. If you can't talk to them, go to a school counselor, a pastor, a neighbor, or a friend.

DON'T GIVE UP UNTIL YOU GET HELP.

To learn more about depression and finding help, turn to page 116.

The *Paralyzed* Perfectionist

When you're unsure or afraid of where you're going, the safest bet is to go nowhere. When you don't want to risk being wrong, the surest thing to do is nothing. But this should be a temporary state, one you visit only until you're able to make an informed decision. Perfectionists take refuge in inertia. They become mentally and emotionally paralyzed, incapable of exerting themselves.

If you could read the mind of a paralyzed perfectionist, here are some of the rationalizations you might see:

If I never complete that project, I don't have to risk getting a bad grade.

If I never try out, I don't have to risk feeling bad when I don't make the team.

If I never apply for that job, I don't have to risk the chance they'll choose someone else instead.

If I never write that short story/paint that picture/perform that piece of music I composed/submit that poem for publication, I don't have to risk being rejected or criticized.

What are the two most noticeable words all these statements have in common? *Never* and *risk*. Many psychologists believe that constantly pushing kids to excel, always focusing on their performance, creates children who are afraid to take risks and fearful of not getting the approval they've learned to appreciate. Many teachers are concerned over the number of bright students who spend their school years calmly and obediently taking notes and following the rules—never questioning, never challenging, never speaking out, taking less-challenging courses to protect their GPA.

There was once a shy writer who completed a huge manuscript but was afraid to turn it in to a publisher. What if no one accepted it? She wasn't sure she could take being turned down. Today there are thirty million copies of her book in print, around the world and in several languages. Her name was Margaret Mitchell; her book, *Gone with the Wind*.

Check It Out !

Do It Now! Break the Procrastination Habit by Dr. William J. Knaus and John W. Edgerly (New York: John Wiley & Sons, 1997). Focuses on how to identify the causes of your procrastination and find solutions to overcome it.

It's About Time! The Six Styles of Procrastination and How to Overcome Them by Dr. Linda Sapadin with Jack Maguire. (New York: Penguin, 1997). A quiz helps readers determine what kind of procrastinator they are, and a three-pronged approach to change helps them learn new habits.

Procrastination Research Group
www.carleton.ca/~tpychyl
This site provides much helpful information about procrastination, along with links to other significant sites that focus on this topic.

3

What Perfectionism Does to Your Body

The battle to keep up appearances unnecessarily, the mask—whatever name you give creeping perfectionism—robs us of our energies.

—Robin Worthington

On the outside, perfectionism looks a lot like the pursuit of excellence, but on the inside it bears little resemblance. Perfectionists take things to the extreme, and that's where problems start. Excellent isn't good enough. Perfectionists tend to take on more and more activities and squeeze them into shorter and shorter time periods, thinking they can beat the clock. In addition to anxiety, hopelessness, and depression, they are prone to stress-related illnesses from overloading their circuits and not getting enough rest. And in their efforts to do more, to look beautiful, to meet the high expectations they face every day, perfectionists sometimes take their stress out on their bodies.

Driving Yourself into the Ground

In today's global economy, exceptional productivity and high-quality results are very important. Businesses try to beat the competition by promising their customers more products, better service, low prices, and speedy delivery. They expect their employees to be committed to their jobs and to a strong work ethic. This means that people often work long hours under intense pressure to meet tight deadlines—with work that needs to meet rigid standards. It means that individuals must continually perform at a very high level.

In *The Overworked American,* economist Juliet Schor notes that over the past two decades the average worker has added an extra 164 hours—a whole month on the job—to the work year. For many people, making a living leaves little time or energy for family activities or a personal life. Countless families deal with a difficult set of circumstances: work pressures, a severe lack of time, financial concerns, and two-earner families. In 1950, 12.6 percent of married mothers who had children under the age of seventeen worked for pay. By 1994, the percentage had risen to 69 percent! Needless to say, this increase in hours worked can lead to an increase in life stress. Absenteeism, high turnover, on-the-job accidents, stress-related illnesses, and other effects cause major economic problems all over the world.

While workplaces and schools tend to reward perfectionist behavior—the long hours, the tendency to skip vacations, the "perfect" results—being a perfectionist can be unhealthy. Perfectionists seem especially apt to become stressed by increasing demands, and they tend to suffer the physical problems of stress more than nonperfectionists. A 1994 study of 9,000 managers—18 percent of whom considered themselves perfectionists—found that the perfectionists reported a 75 percent higher illness rate (including gastrointestinal ailments, headaches, cardiovascular problems, and depression) than did their colleagues.

Working for a perfectionist can likewise be a stressful and unproductive experience. To a perfectionist boss, a job is never done well enough. And a supervisor who can't forgive his or her own mistakes is less likely to have sympathy for others' errors. He or she may hold unrealistic expectations for employees' dedication to the job, while at the same time, be unwilling to trust the staff to do the work.

These issues are so widespread that local agencies and high schools, such as top-rated New Trier high school in Winnetka, Illinois, now offer seminars for adults on work-family conflict. Balancing the demands of school, work, and family is a rigorous challenge—especially for perfectionists.

"Speeding" Toward Trouble: Caffeine and Other Drugs

Have you ever wanted to stay awake when your brain and body told you it was time for bed? Have you ever felt that you had to stay awake—to study for a test, or finish a paper, or complete a project or presentation you were determined to get done before the morning?

Of course you have. We all have. Everyone gets behind on occasion, and everyone stays up too late once in a while, maybe even pulling an all-nighter.

For perfectionists, though, this can turn into a regularly scheduled event—especially if they combine their perfectionism with procrastination. They wait until the last minute to start something that will take hours to do. Then, when their heads start nodding over their desks, they reach for help.

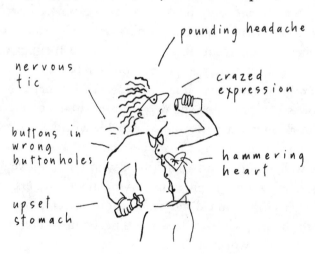

Coffee. Tea. Sodas. Over-the-counter stay-awake pills. These are the constant companions of the procrastinating perfectionist. The ingredient they all have in common is caffeine.

Caffeine is an odorless, slightly bitter drug that acts as a stimulant to the nervous system. It increases your heart rate and rhythm, affects your circulatory system, and increases urination. It also stimulates the secretion of stomach acids. Small amounts of caffeine can make you feel more alert and think more clearly for a short time. Too much can make you nervous, jittery, and cranky and upset your stomach.

Caffeine causes your body to release internal "stress signals." That's why you can hear your heart beating and feel your adrenaline pumping. Normally your body behaves like that only when you're running away from something scary or climbing a mountain or performing some other fairly strenuous physical activity. Over a prolonged period of time, high caffeine intake can lead to ulcers, insomnia, high blood pressure, heart irregularities, heart disease, and delirium.

Caffeine may be hidden in all sorts of products—cold pills, pain relievers, diet pills, chocolate, ice cream—and it has another big downside. It's addictive. Once you start using caffeine, you'll need more of it to get the same effects. The lift it provides is short-lived, and when it wears off, you feel even more tired and let down than you did before. The symptoms of withdrawal—headache, depression, and fatigue—can be very unpleasant.

Caffeine has one thing going for it: at least it's legal. (One company has taken advantage of this to make a cola called Jolt with 5.9 milligrams caffeine per ounce—just under the limits considered acceptable by the Food and Drug Administration.)

There are other drugs that aren't legal, and some procrastinating perfectionists resort to these.

Truck drivers going on long runs have been known to take amphetamines, or "speed," to keep from falling asleep behind the wheel. Students studying for exams have been known to take them, too.

Amphetamines obtained without a prescription are illegal. But that's not the only reason to avoid them. They're dangerous, they're habit-forming, and their effects can be unpredictable.

One student took speed to get through the night before an important three-hour exam. He managed to stay up all night studying, but the next day was a disaster. His body was awake, but he was nervous and edgy and had trouble concentrating. He had to read the test questions several times to understand them, and his hands shook, making writing difficult. The time was up before he could finish taking the exam.

Healthy, well-rested, chemical-free people feel better, look better, and perform better.

5 Safe Ways to Stay Awake

You've got to hand that paper in tomorrow morning at 9:00 sharp. Or you've got to study for that exam. No two ways about it—it's now or never. Resist the urge to make a pot of coffee. Instead, try one or more of these healthy alternatives:

Get physical. Run in place, do sit-ups or jumping jacks, whatever. Exercise gets your heart pumping and moves oxygen-rich blood through your circulatory system. Plus it makes you feel better. After five or ten minutes of hopping around, you'll sit back down at your desk with pink cheeks and renewed energy.

Turn on some stimulating music. Sousa marches may be going too far, but rousing popular music, a classical variety, or bouncy jazz may be just the ticket to get you energized. Some students report that working to music actually improves their concentration because it shuts out other extraneous noises.

Eat something crunchy and good for you. Try a carrot, an apple, some celery sticks with peanut butter. Maybe your body needs a boost. (But stay away from sugar, which gives you a quick rush and then sends you crashing down again.) Why crunchy? Because the noise you make chewing might help keep you awake!

Relax and focus your mind. When you find your thoughts becoming scattered, take a break. Find a comfortable place to sit; keep your spine straight; stare at a spot on the wall, or close your eyes; breathe slowly, deeply, and rhythmically; and think the same syllable, word, or short phrase over and over again. (Like listening to music, that has the effect of masking outside noises.) Whenever you find your mind wandering away from your syllable, word, or phrase, get back on track with it. After about ten minutes of this, you should be able to return to work with a clear head.

Take a catnap. Set your alarm for a half-hour or an hour, and then curl up under the covers and go to sleep. Even this short period of rest will give your body and brain a chance to recharge. (The trick is to make sure that you get up when your alarm goes off!)

The Eating Disorders Dilemma

When doctors and scientists study young people with eating disorders, they often find a common characteristic: perfectionism. Perfectionism doesn't cause eating disorders, but there does seem to be a connection.

One recognized cause of eating disorders is the emphasis our culture places on the need to be thin at any cost. Television, advertising, and the movies constantly send the message that thin is in. The most popular models, actors, dancers, and musicians are slender, and if they're not, you can bet critics will comment. We've all heard the saying "You can never be too rich or too thin," and many of us believe it. We equate thinness with physical perfection.

There are three specific types of eating disorders: anorexia nervosa, bulimia nervosa, and compulsive eating. People who have one of these three disorders commonly place an abnormal emphasis on eating, food, and body shape.

■ **Anorexics** literally starve themselves through obsessive dieting, eating very little, or refusing to eat at all. They're so fearful of being fat that nothing can convince them to risk gaining weight. They may make themselves vomit after eating or take diuretics or laxatives to keep their weight down.

- **Bulimics** "binge and purge," stuffing themselves with huge amounts of food and then trying to compensate by forcing themselves to vomit, misusing laxatives, fasting, or exercising excessively.

- **Compulsive eaters** binge eat. They are caught in a cycle of shame and emotional pain: binge eat, gain weight, diet, feel miserable while dieting, break the diet and feel guilty about it, find relief and comfort in eating, regain any lost weight (plus some), and diet again.

All of the disorders are harmful, although anorexia is considered the most dangerous. According to the American Anorexia/Bulimia Association, an estimated 1 percent of adolescents and young adults suffer from anorexia and up to 10 percent of these will die from starvation, suicide, or electrolyte imbalance. About 3 to 5 percent of adolescents and young adults suffer from bulimia. Mary Pipher, Ph.D., asserts that the problem is even more widespread. In her book *Reviving Ophelia* she states that "on any given day in America, half our teenage girls are dieting and one in five young women has an eating disorder." While eating disorders occur in both sexes, females seem to be more susceptible than males. According to the National Institute of Mental Health, 90 percent of those with eating disorders are adolescent women.

Anorexia and bulimia have difficult and dangerous side-effects, including hypothermia, dehydration, insomnia, constipation, hair loss, and unclear thinking; women may find that their menstrual cycles become irregular or stop altogether. Excessive vomiting may damage the esophagus and teeth, since vomiting brings up stomach acids. In extreme cases victims may experience damage to vital organs and heart failure.

Anorexia and bulimia are complex disorders that operate on physical, emotional, and mental levels, which makes them especially hard to treat. It's tough to convince people with anorexia that they need help. They often remain convinced that they're "too fat," even when their ribs are sticking out and they're too weak to get out of bed. And bulimics usually binge and purge in secret.

Athletes, especially those who engage in sports where thinness appeals to judges, are in particular danger of anorexia and bulimia. According to studies by psychologist Donald Williamson of Louisiana State University, women in "lean" sports such as figure skating and gymnastics have significantly higher rates of eating disorders (around 4 percent) than women in "nonlean" sports like basketball and soccer (approaching zero).

According to Williamson, "Several risk factors interact to increase a female athlete's risk of developing an eating disorder. She perceives pressure from her sport and coach to be thin; she judges her performance negatively; and she feels anxious about her performance. These three risk factors lead to an exaggerated dissatisfaction with body size and shape."

For example, in 1988 at a meet in Budapest, a U.S. judge told Christy Henrich, a world-class gymnast, that she was too heavy and needed to lose weight if she expected to make the 1992 Olympics in Barcelona. Henrich became obsessed about her weight. She became anorexic. Training nine hours a day, she sometimes ate only a slice of apple all day. At one point, her weight fell to 47 pounds. Eventually, she became too weak to perform the grueling routines required of high-class gymnasts and was forced to retire at eighteen. She never did reach the Olympics. On July 26, 1994, anorexia took Henrich's life.

Studies with male athletes support Williamson's findings. Men participating in sports that emphasize a certain weight or physique, such as body building and wrestling, tend to develop eating disorders more often than men in other sports.

"Gymnastics doesn't cause eating disorders," says sports psychologist Joan L. Duda, Ph.D., of Purdue University. "There's nothing about the balance beam or uneven bars that makes a girl develop a dysfunctional relationship with food. Instead, it's a motivation-related question and a lack-of-information problem."

To research this, Duda and nutritionist Dan Benardot of Georgia State University worked with the U.S. Gymnastics

Association to conduct four studies on elite and pre-elite gym-nasts. The researchers found that "a training climate that empha-sizes winning above all else predicted low self-esteem, negative body image, a lower degree of enjoyment and a higher degree of stress associated with competing." These are the same triggers that Williamson and others have linked to an increased risk of eating disorders.

Treatment for eating disorders may include counseling, psy-chotherapy, family therapy, behavior modification, medication, and hospitalization. It's time-consuming and challenging but effective. Patients often strongly resist treatment; family members feel guilty and frustrated.

For perfectionists, eating disorders are another side of the "all-or-nothing" mind-set. The more you focus on being perfect, the more aware you become of your faults. Feelings of worth-lessness set in. Especially if you think you're being dominated in other areas of your life—family, school, work—you may decide to take charge of at least one area: eating. Controlling and monitoring your food intake is something you can do.

As a teen, ballerina Gelsey Kirkland periodically starved herself. Later, she learned to vomit to keep her weight down. Though five feet four inches tall, she weighed less than 100 pounds. In her autobiography, *Dancing on My Grave*, she talks about her own pursuit of the body beautiful.

Several other famous women have made their own bouts with eating disorders public. Actors Jane Fonda and Ally Sheedy, gymnasts Kathy Johnson and Nadia Comaneci, and dancer Paula Abdul all have talked about their struggles.

Many people with eating disorders admit to feeling pressured to be "the perfect person." Some lay the blame on parental expectations, while others point the finger at society and themselves. Often they share a deep fear of making mistakes and a low sense of self-esteem.

Eating disorders are a deadly way to try to gain control over your life. It's worth learning more about them. If you feel you need more information right away, you can contact any of the following:

National Association of Anorexia Nervosa and Associated Disorders (ANAD)
P.O. Box 7
Highland Park, IL 60035
(847) 831-3438
www.anad.org
This self-help organization has chapters or groups in most states.

National Eating Disorders Association
603 Stewart Street, Suite 803
Seattle, WA 98101
(206) 382-3587
www.nationaleatingdisorders.org
Call, write, or log on to their Web site for comprehensive information from this organization.

American Psychological Association
750 First Street NE
Washington, DC 20002-4242
1-800-374-2721
www.apa.org
Staff will send out information on a confidential basis or provide a
referral source to someone in your area.

Self-Harm

Perfectionism can also take a toll on the body in other ways.
Some perfectionists purposefully take their frustration, anxiety,
and sense of worthlessness out on their bodies. Cutting, or self-
mutilation, means injuring yourself using razor blades, needles,
knives, shards of glass, or other objects. Some people who do this
make shallow cuts on the skin; others inflict deep wounds that
can be life-threatening.

Why would anyone do this? Armando Favazza, a professor at
the University of Missouri at Columbia Medical School, says the
short answer is that it provides temporary relief from painful
symptoms such as anxiety and desperation.

More often than not, cutters are female, but males too are
susceptible. From the outside, they may look just like anybody
else and can be found anywhere: affluent or poor neighbor-
hoods, private schools, juvenile detention centers, colleges and
universities, the workplace.

Perhaps the most well-known example of someone who
struggled with self-injury is the late Princess Diana. In a BBC
television interview in 1995, she said, "You have so much pain
inside yourself that you try and hurt yourself on the outside
because you want help."

In *A Bright Red Scream,* author Marilee Strong explains,
"Cutters are people who use their own skin to change their
moods, to achieve a little-understood state of psychological
awareness through intense pain, and to communicate a message
that until recently has seemed indecipherable."

Strong describes a fourteen-year-old girl who was bingeing, purging, and cutting. "Bingeing numbs out whatever is bothering me," says the teen, "and purging gets rid of it all. When I cut myself, as soon as I see the blood I feel better." The relief of cutting and bulimia is soon replaced by rage and guilt, however. Always the perfectionist, the girl feels that she can't even hurt herself right. "It's so perverse," she says. "I feel embarrassed talking about it. But if I feel that I didn't cut deep enough, or it didn't bleed enough, I feel that I failed and I want to cut more."

A few cutters do stop this damaging practice on their own. It may simply be a matter of "growing out" of a behavior that no longer helps. Others need a variety of help, such as psychotherapy, psychoanalysis, drugs, or a combination of approaches. If the cutter does not come to terms with the underlying reasons for the behavior, he or she may not be able to abandon it.

In severe cases, teens may need to be placed in an adolescent psychiatric unit. As improvement is made, outpatient care can be established.

Check It Out !

A Bright Red Scream by Marilee Strong (New York: Penguin Putnam Inc., 1999). An insightful and informative discussion of cutting, also known as self-mutilation.

Dancing on My Grave: An Autobiography by Gelsey Kirkland (New York: Berkley Publications Group, 1996). One of America's most famous ballerinas tells the story of her battle with anorexia.

Drugs & Your Brain by Beatrice R. Grabish (New York: Rosen Publishing, 1998). The book presents Tanya's story of drug addiction. Also included is informational background about a healthy brain, the brain on drugs, and where and how to get help for drug addictions.

Fighting Invisible Tigers: A Stress Management Guide for Teens by Earl Hipp (Minneapolis: Free Spirit Publishing, 1995). Covering topics like building relationships, making decisions, dealing with fears, and taking risks, the author offers a variety of stress management and life management skills to teens.

Food Fight by Janet Bode (New York: Simon and Schuster, 1998). Filled with first-person stories from affected young people and their parents and helpful information from doctors, nutritionists, psychologists, and other experts in the field.

Eating Disorders & Food Addiction Resources
www.open-mind.org/Directory
An A to Z listing of links to information about eating disorders.

Internet Mental Health
www.mentalhealth.com
Links to thousands of online self-help resources on many health issues, including alcohol and drug abuse and eating disorders.

Something Fishy
www.something-fishy.org
Online resources and information about eating disorders.

4

What Perfectionism Does to Your Relationships

> friendship with one's self is all-important,
> because without it one cannot be friends
> with anyone else in the world.
>
> —Eleanor Roosevelt

Like most people, perfectionists need and want the friendship and approval of others. Yet they often have special problems in their family and social relationships. Some perfectionists assume everyone around them expects them to be perfect, and they worry about living up to those expectations.

Being Too Critical of Others

Some perfectionists impose their too-high standards on everyone around them. They believe that their friends, parents, teachers, and siblings ought to be perfect, too. They have a bad habit of criticizing anyone who doesn't live up to their ideal or dares to make mistakes.

The trouble with criticism is that it alienates other people. Nobody likes being on the receiving end, and people who find themselves in that position are likely to run the other way fast.

Let's say you've got a legitimate gripe. You want to get it off your chest, but you're not sure how to do it. In the past you might have tried public humiliation, but you know those tactics don't work. They don't make you feel good either, and you're ready to try something new.

So, what do you do? First of all, avoid criticizing people for *who* and *what* they are. In other words, don't make personal comments. For example, suppose you loan a friend a favorite shirt and it comes back stained. Shouting "You're a big slob with the table manners of an English sheepdog" is no way to open negotiations about the dry-cleaning bill.

Instead, try this three-step approach to problem-solving:

1. Clarify the issue in your own mind before bringing it up with the other person. Figure out what's really bothering you; then separate it out from any unrelated issues (like old gripes or grudges).

2. Tell the other person how you perceive the situation and how you feel about it—without accusing or criticizing. Use I-messages: "I feel angry and upset because . . ." Avoid blanket statements like "You're always doing such-and-such" or "You never do so-and-so."

3. Propose a solution and give the other person the opportunity to do the same—while keeping an open mind.

For example, instead of "You're a big slob," etc., try "I'm glad you brought my shirt back, but I'm angry about the spot. I really want to wear the shirt to my sister's wedding next Saturday. Do you think you could have it cleaned before then?"

Instead of This: "You have a mouth the size of the Grand Canyon and it's obvious I can't trust you anymore. You told Carlo the secret I told you. How could you do such a thing?"

Try This: "Carlo told me something I was sure I told you in confidence. I feel angry and embarrassed. Maybe you didn't realize it was supposed to stay a secret. How can I let you know next time?"

Instead of This: "You stole my idea for the science project. I guess you're too dumb to have ideas of your own, since you're always taking mine."

Try This: "I was surprised when you told the teacher what you plan to do for the science project. It sounded a lot like the idea I told you about last week. If you needed help coming up with an idea, you could have asked me. Then I'd feel comfortable doing the same with you."

Instead of This: "You're totally irresponsible. You promised to meet me at the game and then didn't even show up. You made me miss the whole first quarter."

Try This: "I thought we agreed to meet at the gym at 7:30. I felt silly standing there while everyone else walked past me to get inside. If something comes up the next time we make plans, please call me and let me know."

We could add a fourth and final step to this problem-solving process: forgiveness. In fact, that alone may be all that's necessary in some situations. The friend who goofs or lets you down may need to be told, "That's okay; forget it." Or "Yes, I was really angry (or disappointed) about it, but I'm okay now and we can put it behind us."

The "Perfect" Partner

Nowhere is the desire for "perfect" friends more apparent than when perfectionists go in search of partners—boyfriends and girlfriends.

What do you look for? When it comes to dating someone, what's important to you? For each of the following categories, choose the description from either the A or B column that comes closest to what you want in a partner.

A	Looks	B
■ Gorgeous ■ Great shape ■ Cool clothes ■ A real head-turner		■ Takes pride in his or her appearance ■ Comfortable with his or her style

A   Brains   B

A	B
■ Honors program only, please	■ Knows about many different subjects
■ Devastating wit	■ Curious
■ At least as smart as I am	■ Interested in things I don't know much about

A   Popularity   B

A	B
■ In the "in" crowd	■ Liked and respected by others
■ Homecoming royalty	■ Knows how to make and keep friends
■ Captain of the team	■ Doesn't try to exclude others
■ Valedictorian	
■ Invited to the best parties	

A   Personality   B

A	B
■ Outgoing	■ Likes serious conversation
■ Always a riot to be with	■ Wants to learn about me
■ The life of the party	■ Doesn't talk unless there's something to say

A   Interests   B

A	B
■ In the "hot" clubs	■ Involved in the community
■ Always at games	■ Campaigns for political candidates
■ Prom committee	■ Volunteers at the local hospital
■ Exceptional athlete	
■ Student government	

You can probably see a pattern here. Column A descriptions deal with more superficial characteristics often dependent on popular opinion, while those in Column B focus more on inner qualities—the things that may not be as obvious and aren't as closely tied to what other people think.

The point is to ask yourself what you really want—and why. Have you decided that you'll only go out with straight-A students, or class officers, or the most popular students, or the best looking ones? What about someone who's kind of shy, not too popular, and not a genius but seems interested in you? Are you willing to give that person a chance? How do you treat people who aren't as "good" as you are? Do you just tolerate them, or do you make a genuine effort to get to know them and let them get to know you?

It's natural to want to date attractive people. But if that's your only goal, you're bound to be frustrated and disappointed. It's when we learn to see what's under the surface that we stand the best chance of developing relationships that are meaningful, satisfying, and long-lasting.

If we accept the images the media say are important to relationships, it's hard to be ourselves and accept other people as they are, blemishes and all. Very few of us resemble top models or actors. Very few of us can afford to dress as expensively or pay that much attention to our appearance. Yet the media continue to project the image that appearance is key—not personality, not abilities, not talents, not inner qualities, but looks.

It's natural to want to date people who engage your mind. That way, you're more likely to be able to find things to do and talk about that interest you both. But there are many kinds of intelligence, not all of which show up on quarterly report cards and dean's lists. What about the student who plays in a jazz band? Or a classmate who invents intriguing gadgets in her basement after school? Don't overlook people who can open your eyes to new and interesting worlds.

It's natural to want to date popular people. After all, going out with the class president, lead singer in the band, or the homecoming king or queen reflects on you. But when you limit your choices to a relatively few people (how many class presidents can there be?), you limit your chances to meet everyone else.

What shows isn't always what counts. You get the idea. Take time to talk to the seemingly nondescript person who sits behind you in math class, and you might find someone who takes flying lessons or runs marathons or writes software or knows more about cars than NASCAR racer Jeff Gordon. You'll never know unless you bother to find out.

There are plenty of nice people out there who are worth meeting and spending time with.

It's natural to want to date people you feel good around. Another mistake perfectionists make is expecting always to feel great when they're with their boyfriends or girlfriends. But trying to turn a relationship into an all-or-nothing proposition is unrealistic. It doesn't allow for off-days, mood shifts, and the ups and downs that are a normal part of everyday life and just being human.

Most of us grew up on fairy tales and movies in which the handsome prince and beautiful princess meet, overcome all obstacles together, and then marry and live "happily ever after." Sadly, there is no such thing. Relationships take persistent work, and some of it isn't much fun. We have to be honest with others, and we have to be willing to listen when they're honest with us, even when it hurts.

It's also unrealistic to expect another person to be your whole life. Many young couples fall into this trap, getting so wrapped up in each other that they shut out the rest of the world and let their other friendships lapse. Even when you do find someone who seems right for you, it's important that you both maintain your own interests, activities, and friendships. (Besides, doing so makes you more interesting.)

When perfectionists do find that special someone, they may have a harder-than-usual time getting close. Perfectionists are reluctant to show their emotions and share information about themselves because they're afraid of letting others see their imperfections. Getting close means taking risks and allowing people to know the real you—including the insecure and less-than-perfect parts.

> A perfectionist is a sure cure for happiness.
>
> —Lorraine Colletti-Lafferty

Some people carry their perfectionism into their emotional life, telling themselves their relationship isn't any good if they're not 100 percent happy in it all of the time. It's okay to admit to being unsure, or worried, or even afraid. It's okay to show anger and frustration and disappointment.

It's also okay to let your guard down in front of a friend. When you do, you're communicating your trust and confidence in that person. And that tends to make friendships stronger.

Perfectionists are also prone to thinking they can change the people they get involved with. They seem to believe that others are "bound" to improve in their company—and they're all too willing to start the improvement campaign. "Let me make a suggestion" turns into "Do it my way." And "I hope you don't mind my telling you this, but . . ." is a sneaky way of saying, "Be the person I want you to be."

One young woman was so badgered by her boyfriend that she seriously considered suicide. "He was a perfectionist, and nothing I did ever pleased him," Lara remembers. "I kept trying to meet his standards, but I never could. It drove me so crazy that I actually wrote a suicide note. Halfway through it I realized what I was doing and knew it was time to get out of the relationship. Now I look for people who accept who I am."

Overcommitment

Another problem many perfectionists have is the tendency to overcommit themselves and be super-responsible. They spend time on schoolwork, music lessons, athletic training, volunteer committees, college applications, part-time jobs—everything but their relationships. Overcommitment may be a way of avoiding closeness, and it may signal the need to reevaluate your priorities. It's important to keep your grades up, get involved in outside activities, and follow through on your promises and obligations. But it's also important to be there for your friends when they need you—especially if you expect the same from them.

The "Perfect" Family

When perfectionists have problems in their relationships, it's seldom their fault alone. For many, the trouble starts at home with parents who want them to have "perfect" friends—meaning friends who meet their expectations.

Like the rest of us, parents sometimes forget that everyone has faults and blemishes, seen and unseen. While they usually do want what's best for their children, they can make mistakes. (Remember that they can also be right on occasion!)

Generally speaking, parents appreciate openness and knowing what's going on in their children's lives. It's when they're kept in the dark or surprised that they're apt to clamp down or make demands that seem unreasonable. If you want your parents to be more accepting of the friends you choose for yourself, here are some guidelines that might help:

- Talk to them about the things you and your friends do together and why you enjoy being with them.

- Try to respect and live within the boundaries your parents set for you. If they decide that certain places and activities are off limits, don't just march off and do as you please. If they say no to something that's really important to you, present your case as calmly and objectively as you can. ("I know you don't like the pizza parlor. But that's where the yearbook club has decided to meet on Thursdays after school, and I really want to participate.")

- Don't keep your friends a secret—let your parents meet them. Spend time with them at your house; invite them to dinner; give your parents a chance to see them and talk with them. It's easier for parents to accept the known than the unknown. Unless you plan to run off and join a gang, you should be able to pick your own friends.

Siblings

You may be able to choose your friends, but when it comes to your siblings, you're stuck with what you get. And sometimes parents unwittingly make things harder.

Even parents who know better can't help comparing their children. When they do it aloud, however, they fuel the fires of sibling rivalry. And when even one child is a high-performance perfectionist, it can cause a rift that may take years to heal.

Siblings resent being measured against a brother or sister who seems to do everything right. As fifteen-year-old Andy reports, "My brother gets mad when Mom and Dad brag about my grades." Sheila, fourteen, feels cut off from her sisters: "My parents call me 'the brain' and tell my sisters they should be more like me. It's as if I'm the special one and they're not as important. That's not true, and I wish my parents would realize that I need to be a part of the family—not apart from it."

Wow, I didn't know you could do _that_... and you taught the cat, too?

"My older brother got everything he wanted," Lauri, thirty, remembers. "He was a top athlete and made the varsity tennis and basketball teams his freshman year. Mom went to all his games. I played intramural volleyball, and she usually skipped my meets because they weren't 'real' competitions."

What can you do if your parents are being insensitive? You can try talking to them about it—always a good place to start. Maybe they honestly don't realize the effects of what they're doing. (For ideas on talking with parents, see pages 108–112.)

You can also work extra hard at getting along with your siblings. Resist the temptation to remind them of how smart you are (even in the middle of an argument). Don't rub it in every time you succeed at something. Be sure to notice their achievements, and remain open to letting them show you a thing or two.

Finally, you can let them know that you don't like it when your parents compare them to you—that it makes you uncomfortable, too. Besides, it puts you in the position of having to be perfect all the time. They may think it feels good to spend your life on a pedestal, but it gets pretty lonely at the top.

Amazing—but True!

If you want your parents to listen to you, you're not alone! The Colorado Psychiatric Society created the following essay topic for their statewide contest for high school students:

Teenagers today continue to be the victims of psychiatric crises—suicide, depression, eating disorders and drug addiction, to name a few. What are the issues behind this that adults need to understand in order to be of more help?

The Society expected to hear about the dangers of peer pressure or about how parents interfere in the lives of kids. Instead, the nearly universal response was "We want our parents to listen to us." As one student wrote, "Just talk to me. . . . Make time in your busy schedule to learn more about me."[1]

Another study of 133 families found that youths who have close relationships with their parents are more likely to be emotionally healthy than other youths. The study also found that close family relationships help prepare teens for increasing independence.[2]

---

1. Scripps Howard News Service, Minneapolis *Star Tribune,* July 21, 1997.

2. *Journal of Early Adolescence* 16 (1996): 274–300.

Check It Out !

Don't Sweat the Small Stuff with Your Family: Simple Ways to Keep Loved Ones and Household Chaos from Taking Over Your Life by Richard Carlson, Ph.D. (New York: Hyperion, 1998). Short essays show readers how to avoid becoming overwhelmed by life—particularly from those closest to them.

What Teens Need to Succeed by Peter L. Benson, Ph.D.; Judy Galbraith, M.A.; and Pamela Espeland (Minneapolis: Free Spirit Publishing, 1998). Easy-to-understand tips and suggestions help you take charge of your own destiny.

Why Am I Afraid to Tell You Who I Am? by John Powell (Allan, TX: Tabor Publishing, 1995). Discover why you are the way you are and how you can get to be who you really want to be.

Camp Fire USA
www.CampFire.org
This nationwide organization offers mentoring and service learning opportunities, among many other programs.

Character Counts!
www.charactercounts.org
This national nonprofit organization focuses on building character traits: respect, fairness, trustworthiness, and citizenship.

Child Trends, Inc.
www.childtrends.org
Current data and research on children and teens.

Girl Scouts of the U.S.A.
www.girlscouts.org
The world's largest organization for girls, Girl Scouts provides a safe, supportive way for girls to participate in projects involving computers and technology, careers, the environment, personal finance, and sports.

5

How to Ease Up
on Yourself

The more you praise and celebrate your life,
the more there is in life to celebrate.
The more you complain, the more you find fault,
the more misery and fault you will have to find.

—Oprah Winfrey

Now that you know some of the problems of perfectionism, it seems only logical to remedy or avoid them. Since most of the pressure perfectionists feel comes from inside, a good place to begin is by easing up on yourself.

Maybe you need a role model or two to start you on your way. Think of someone you admire. If you can find a biography of that person, read it. Also do an Internet search. Try to find out what your role model's life was really like. And in the process, you'll probably find out some surprising information. For example, painter Claude Monet, dancer Isadora Duncan, and writer Mark Twain never finished grade school. Composer George Gershwin, newscaster Peter Jennings, actor Carrie Fisher, singers Frank Sinatra and The Artist Formerly Known as Prince, and Bill Gates all dropped out of school.

Emily Dickinson was a recluse. Martin Luther was intolerant of peasants and Jews. Charles Lindbergh was a reckless barnstormer who cracked up four planes before soloing across the

Atlantic. Before World War II, he came out in favor of the Nazis and recommended that the United States fight on the German side. And lots of other famous people stumbled and fumbled their way into the history books.

10 Famous People Who Made It Big Despite a Rocky Start

Louisa May Alcott was told by an editor she'd never write anything popular. More than a century later, her novels are still being read, and many consider *Little Women* one of the best American children's books of the past 200 years.

Florence Chadwick, the first woman to swim the English Channel, also attempted to be the first woman to swim from Catalina Island to the California coast. Caught in thick fog, she had to abandon her try, but only two months later she succeeded, beating the men's record by two hours.

Walt Disney once got fired by a newspaper editor because "he had no good ideas." He went on to create Mickey Mouse, Donald Duck, Walt Disney Pictures (which has won 76 Academy Awards), and Disneyland; his greatest dream, Epcot, opened in 1982.

Louis Freeman, the first African-American chief airline pilot, tried to join the Air Force after graduating from college but failed the required test. Not used to failing, he doubled his efforts, took the test again, and passed.

Charles Goodyear, founder of Goodyear tires, had many business failures and was even sent to debtor's prison before accidentally discovering the vulcanization process that revolutionized the rubber industry.

Steve Jobs, founder of Apple, wasn't successful when he and Steve Wozniak tried to sell the rights to the personal computer they developed. A Hewlett-Packard executive told them, "We don't need you. You haven't got through college yet." The president of Atari said, "Get your feet off my desk, get out of here, you stink, and we're not going to buy your product."

Michael Jordan didn't make the varsity basketball team as a sophomore in high school. Though he was embarrassed and disappointed, this gave him the impetus to work harder to make the team, a standard of excellence he maintained throughout his basketball career.

John F. Kennedy Jr. faced two well-publicized failures to pass the New York bar exam before finally passing on his third try.

Abraham Lincoln started out as a captain at the beginning of the Blackhawk War; by the end of the war, he had been demoted to private.

Marilyn Monroe was told, "You'd better learn secretarial work or else get married" by a modeling agency after her first interview.

What did these people all have in common, in addition to great ability?

They took risks. They took chances again and again. They took their failures in stride and kept on trying. They liked being challenged. They made mistakes and learned from them.

You can, too.

> Even a mistake may turn out to be the one thing necessary to a worthwhile achievement.
>
> —Henry Ford

Learning to Fail

Perfectionists have a hard time taking risks. The fear of failure, of being "imperfect," is so strong, it can be debilitating.

That's why one of the first things you should do to ease up on yourself is to try something new—something you've never done before, and preferably something you might not be very good at. Is there a chance you won't succeed? Of course. You might even look silly. But if you can't do it perfectly, well, that would be perfect.

What's so good about performing badly—or, at least, less than perfectly? Here are just a few of the benefits:

- It gives you a new perspective on yourself and everything else you do. (Falling and picking yourself up to find that the world hasn't ended can be liberating.)

- It gives you the freedom and motivation to strike out in still more untried directions.

- It gives you a better understanding of others. (Whenever you try something outside your own realm, you can't help looking differently at people who know things you don't know and can do things you can't do.)

- It gives you permission to do less than your best at something else—and something else after that.

- It teaches you that there are degrees of accomplishment—that it's not an all-or-nothing proposition. (You don't have to be the best to learn something and have fun.)

- It teaches you that not succeeding can be normal, necessary, even desirable.

Be bold. If you're going to make an error, make a doozey, and don't be afraid to hit the ball.

—Billie Jean King

I've always wanted to learn to fly.

So, what new something should you try? Make a list of things you've always been interested in. What about snowboarding, learning Russian, neon art, designing clothes, vegetarian cooking? What about sailing, sculpting, or the tango? Why not develop a stand-up comedy routine? Anything you decide on will help you expand your horizons, discover more about yourself, stretch your brain, and come up with new criteria for self-assessment.

No matter what you choose, you can't lose.

I think success has no rules, but you can learn a great deal from failures.

—Jean Kerr

Learning to Laugh

Perfectionists, as a rule, take things very seriously. It was probably a perfectionist who coined the phrase "Life is no laughing matter."

If you can't remember the last time you laughed so hard you cried or fell off your chair, you're long overdue. Start with safe things and funny people. (Chances are they won't be perfectionists—an excellent reason all by itself for seeking them out.)

Laughter is by definition healthy.

—Doris Lessing

There are biophysical reasons why laughter makes you feel good. For one, it's terrific exercise. You simply can't keep still while you're laughing. Prolonged belly-laughter affects almost every muscle and most major organs. It increases your respiratory activity and heart rate, stimulates your circulatory system, and reduces stress. Meanwhile your pituitary gland releases chemicals that add to your sense of well-being. Your whole body feels lighter and more relaxed. (Do you remember the scene from the movie *Mary Poppins* where people laughed, floated to the ceiling, and hung there like helium balloons? That's what it's like!)

Norman Cousins—activist, longtime editor of *Saturday Review* magazine, and papal emissary—believed that laughter actually saved his life. Twice diagnosed with near-fatal diseases, he checked into motels and watched the funniest movies he could find. (He loved the Three Stooges.) Both times he emerged feeling better than ever. Cousins wrote books that explored the healing effect a positive attitude can have on even serious illnesses.

The healing power of humor also takes center stage in the movie *Patch Adams*. Robin Williams' character is based on the story of a real-life doctor who enrolls in medical school so that he can develop a new and unorthodox approach to medicine, one that incorporates humor into its very essence. Both the doctor and the film have been very successful.

> When we can begin to take our failures nonseriously, it means we are ceasing to be afraid of them. It is of immense importance to learn to laugh at ourselves.
>
> —Katherine Mansfield

After you've practiced laughing at safe things, be brave and move on to the next stage: laughing at yourself. No derisive snorts or self-effacing giggles, please; we're aiming for honest laughter. What have you got to laugh at? Try to remember the last time you made a really silly mistake. (The longer ago you made it, the sillier it may seem.) Imagine how you looked from the outside. If someone you know had done the same thing, would you have laughed about it?

> During college I was the featured baton twirler at football games. Once I dropped my flaming baton on the field and started a small fire. Several band members marched over the flames in double time until they put the fire out. As they stomped, they kept on playing. While it was one of life's most embarrassing moments, it still makes me laugh.
>
> —Miriam Adderholdt

Here are a few more ways to firm up your funny bone:

- Keep an imaginary library of "laugh tapes" in your head—incidents you've witnessed or been a part of, jokes you've heard, funny scenes from your favorite movies or television shows. Then "play a tape" whenever you need a lift.

- Throw a silly costume party. (An All-Vegetable party? A Come-as-Your-Favorite-Alien dance? A "Brady Bunch" bash?)

- Do a silly arts-and-crafts project. Make a mask and see how goofy you can make it.

- Call the funniest person you know.

Getting Up and Getting Out

Too many all-nighters and too much stress can have a cumulative effect on your body. Laughter alone can't relieve it; what you need is exercise.

Instead of sitting around worrying about your GPA, your cello solo, or the next big game, try getting up and getting out. Widen your circle of friends to include active people. Then go hiking, camping, horseback riding, swimming, rafting, canoeing, rock climbing, skating, biking—anything physical that sounds like fun to you. You'll come home with energy to spare, and your books will still be where you left them.

Whatever you choose, do it for the joy. Camping isn't about identifying every tree in the campground or having state-of-the-art equipment; it's about sleeping on the ground, singing around a fire, roasting marshmallows, and trying to find the latrine in the dark. Nobody has to try out for water-sliding, that sport where everyone looks ridiculous. And a 4.0 average won't be much help the first time you climb into shoes with wheels.

Your fellow perfectionists may not be interested in such activities. Even better, since that will give you the chance to meet new people. Dwayne, fourteen, took a deep breath and joined his school ski club. Until then his only contact with the kids in ski club had been a few hellos in the hall. "They're nice," he says, "and they like having a good time. Plus, nobody cares if I'm not on the ski team. No one's competing. What a relief!"

Leave your competitive self at home. If you turn your new pursuits into contests, you'll defeat their purpose. You don't have to be the best rock climber or the swimmer with the perfect form. You don't have to be the leader or the know-it-all who's read eighteen books on the topic. You'll probably be surprised at how wonderful it feels to relax and just be yourself.

Turning Problems into Opportunities

Any problem becomes more manageable if you take the time to learn about it. Perfectionists know all about hitting the books and digging for facts; why not turn that to your advantage? Study whatever aspect of perfectionism makes things hardest for you.

Are you an overachiever bordering on workaholism? Then read up on workaholism. Find out what doctors and researchers have discovered about its causes and its effects. Imagine that you're a counselor with a workaholic client, devise a treatment plan, and take your own advice!

Are you a procrastinator? Discover how others conquer this tendency. Ask one of your teachers to let you write a paper on it—and turn it in on time.

On the light side, you may want to get in touch with the Procrastinators' Club of America. The Club was founded in 1956 "to promote the fine art of procrastination to nonprocrastinators, to make known the benefits of putting things off until later, to honor those people who have performed exceptional acts of procrastination, and to have fun." Members have protested the War of 1812 and traveled to Spain to request three ships with which to discover America. Meetings are irregular and late. Request a copy of their Last Month's Newsletter, but don't hold your breath waiting for it. Write or call: Procrastinators' Club of America, Inc., P.O. Box 712, Bryn Athyn, PA 19009, (215) 947-9020. If you put off writing, you can also search out fellow procrastinators on the Web, which is full of fun ideas for wasting time you could spend on more worthwhile pursuits.

Are you a perfectionistic young author who suffers from writer's block? Learn all you can about it. Ironically, lots has been written on the subject—by writers, of course. There are entire books and sections of books on writer's block waiting for you at your public library.

In *The Writer's Survival Guide,* author Rachel Simon points out that because writer's block comes from within, you can heal it only from within. "Writing works a lot like the seasons: You do tremendous work at some times, producing insightful, exciting creations that seem as if they will keep writing themselves forever. Then your energy tapers off, or your ideas come to feel rigid and dry. You enter a phase of not writing, or simply sitting around, feeling dark. And then—*voilà!*—something spins back into place, and you can get going again."

Her solution? "Write something else. It doesn't matter what. Letters to correspondents. A journal, fairy tales for your kids. Your mother's words, verbatim, about how she met your father. Haiku. Content doesn't matter. Beauty of language doesn't matter. Just write anything that appeals to you. Eventually, you'll write your way into a place where you've never been before. Whatever it is, it's still writing. In other words, if you can't do it at all, try some other it. You might find it's just as worthwhile as your original goal, if not more so."

Never underestimate the power of a challenging assignment to get you excited and lead to solutions. If there's one thing perfectionists are really good at, it's leaving no stone unturned. In their push to make sure to get everything right, they do a thorough job of gathering information and ferreting out facts.

> When I discovered that my biggest problem was perfectionism, I decided to tackle it head-on. I made it the subject of my doctoral dissertation. I even wrote a book about it; you're reading it right now.
>
> —Miriam Adderholdt

Check It Out !

Don't Sweat the Small Stuff . . . And It's All Small Stuff by Dr. Richard Carlson (New York: Hyperion, 1997). Helps readers focus on the good parts of their lives and keep the other areas in proper perspective.

Real Kids Taking the Right Risks: Plus How You Can, Too! by Arlene Erlbach (Minneapolis: Free Spirit Publishing, 1998). Twenty first-person profiles and guidelines for taking safe and healthy risks.

Write Where You Are: How to Use Writing to Make Sense of Your Life by Caryn Mirriam-Goldberg, Ph.D. (Minneapolis: Free Spirit Publishing, 1999). Helps teens articulate and understand their hopes and fears, lives and possibilities through writing.

The Page of Procrastination
www.angelfire.com/mi/psociety
A humorous guide to various aspects of procrastination.

6

Perfectionism in Young Women and Men

> Women share with men the need for personal
> success, even the taste for power, and no longer
> are willing to satisfy those needs through the
> achievements of surrogates, whether husbands,
> children, or merely role models.
>
> —Elizabeth Dole

It's no secret that females traditionally have been raised to be less assertive, more accepting, and more complacent than males. And it's no secret that many boys and young men have been taught they should keep a tight rein on their emotions and handle their problems on their own. Gender expectations become fiercely ingrained. Despite progress over the past decades, society is slow to change. Parents, teachers, coaches, and the media all continue to treat boys and girls differently and expect different things of them, and children tend to mirror these expectations.

Because of gender expectations, perfectionism sometimes looks a bit different in males and females—not in its effects or thought patterns, but in how it plays out in their lives. Traditionally, perfectionism in girls and young women could be seen in their striving for perfection in their appearance and in their relationships with family and friends. Perfectionism in boys and young men has been frequently linked to performance in school, the workplace, and athletics.

Society may be changing, but these tendencies linger. Most women are now employed, striving to succeed at home and at work. Men, too, can get caught between conflicting expectations: between new laws and business policies set up to give workers more time for their families, and perceptions that if they do take advantage of these changes, then they aren't serious about their careers. For perfectionists, this can be frustrating as they strive to reach impossible goals in all areas of their lives.

For Girls: Superkid to Superwoman

Girls and young women get many mixed messages from society. They are encouraged to excel academically and athletically, but if they are too successful, they may pay a penalty socially. They sometimes get labeled geeky or "unfeminine." Many boys are intimidated by girls who are smart and strong, and there are always people who resent others' success.

Some girls become trapped between the desire for success and the fear of failure. And when they also have perfectionist tendencies, they can overbook and stretch themselves to their limits, trying to do everything at once and do it all well.

During her junior year in high school Cynthia woke up one day and realized that she was an officer in five school clubs and president of her class, juggling a full load of accelerated courses, and participating in after-school piano, dance, and French lessons. She pulled the covers over her head and wailed, "How did this happen to me?" She managed to make it to the end of the year, which was also nearly the end of her rope. Afraid to disappoint the people who were counting on her, she pushed herself to her limits. She became depressed, physically and emotionally exhausted, and took little pleasure in activities she should have enjoyed.

It's great to be able to do many things well, but overdoing it to the point of being overstressed and worn out is taking it too far. Prolonged stress is dangerous to your emotional and physical health. Taking on more than you can handle can be scary. You may find yourself unable to do your best work or even perform competently. In trying to do everything, you may end up doing nothing you can be proud of.

> Knowing what you can not do is more important than knowing what you can do.
>
> —Lucille Ball

There are times when it's essential to look out for Number 1. That's not being selfish; it's taking care of yourself. Looking at your own needs means taking time to rest, recuperate, and review after finishing one set of projects and before starting the next. That means slowing down, calming down, and taking stock of where you are and where you really want to go.

Thanks in large part to feminism, girls and young women today are more assertive and outspoken than ever before. And they have more choices. Opportunities once closed to their mothers and grandmothers, whether due to legal restrictions or social conventions, are open to young women growing up today. They can become soldiers, teachers, biochemists, mothers, sculptors, nurses, legislators, professional athletes, inventors, administrative assistants, or landscape architects.

The women's movement has tried to give both women and men the freedom to make choices about how they will live and work. Ironically, some people interpret these options as putting extra pressure on women to perform—to continue to be the traditional perfect nurturer and homemaker while now also excelling in a high-powered career. But success doesn't mean being "perfect" in all areas of life (or in any one area). Rather, it's about taking advantage of opportunities to develop your talents and interests wherever you choose—whether at home or in the workplace, whether single or as a family.

For decades, television ads and programs have implied that women must have "perfect" houses, cook "perfect" meals for their "perfect" husbands, look "perfect" at all times, and raise "perfect" children. In recent years, these images have been expanded to include being "perfect" at work, competing with men and other women in the workplace, and climbing the corporate ladder as fast as possible. Young women look ahead and wonder, "Can I do it?" Many feel unequal to the monumental task of doing it all.

But we know that's not possible in reality. Women can't do it all at once very effectively, and neither can men. No one should be expected to. And you can start learning now how to keep your life in balance.

Even superhero Xena, Warrior Princess, never has to take on the daily responsibilities of a family. Intent on her mission to right the wrongs of the world of classical antiquity, she doesn't have to plan twenty-one meals a week, pack school lunches, do the laundry, and go to PTA meetings.

It's not too soon to start thinking about how you want to live your life and where you want to focus your energy. Where you want to be in five years, or ten, or twenty? Remember, you're not necessarily making plans—you're simply exploring possibilities. You may want to talk to your school guidance counselor. Then talk to adult women you know and admire—teachers, neighbors, your mom. Learn about the choices other women are making. Ask a librarian to point you toward books and articles about women. Check out the large numbers of career books now available. You can make more informed decisions once you know what options exist.

You can also observe the boys and men you know to see how they handle competing demands on their time. Maybe you've heard your father say, "I'm sorry; I can't do that right now. I'm already doing as much as I have time for." Or maybe you've overheard a brother or male friend turn down an invitation because he wanted an evening to sit around. Have you ever noticed that men seldom sound apologetic when they refuse a request?

There's something else to be learned from males: the ability to express anger. Studies show that although boys and girls have the same rate of depression during childhood, at age fourteen, suddenly twice as many girls as boys suffer from clinical depression. We don't know exactly why this is. The physical changes of puberty and the struggle with identity and self-esteem are probably involved. Other theories suggest that girls and women turn their anger inward while boys and men express theirs outwardly. Society still accepts angry outbursts in males more so than in females. Many boys vent their feelings in a blast and then go on as if nothing has happened, while more girls tend to stew for days or weeks or months.

Next time you feel put-upon by other people's expectations, try letting them know how you feel. Say, "I'm angry!" and then do something to let your anger out. Jog around the block, yank weeds out of the garden, pound a pillow. (It sounds silly, but it works.)

You can also practice expressing some of the other uncomfortable feelings you may keep locked inside—jealousy, fear, sadness, anxiety, and doubt. Talk with a close friend or an adult you trust, perhaps a parent, other relative, spiritual adviser, club leader or school counselor.

Regardless of any internal or societal expectations you may feel, you don't have to be happy, cheerful, and smiling all the time. Many girls are still brought up believing that this is how they should behave in any and all circumstances. But that's not a healthy way to live. You're entitled to be as grumpy as your brother, as gloomy as your dad, as grouchy as your boyfriend sometimes is—as long as that's the way you really feel. People may be surprised by the new you, but don't let that stop you. They'll get used to it; give them time.

For Boys: Superkid to Superman

Parents, teachers, and other caregivers have expectations for boys as well as girls. Boys are expected to excel at physical risk-taking and active pursuits: winning races, jumping the farthest, smashing the baseball out of the park, hitting the bulls-eye, barreling down a mountain on a snowboard. They are teased for refusing a fight, for showing their softer side, for showing their emotions or paying too much attention to other people's feelings—in short, for acting "like girls."

Men in our society face the expectation that they will protect and support a family someday. To do this, they must be rugged, strong, and competitive—after all, it's a jungle out there. Where female perfectionists may focus first on their appearance, their relationships, and pleasing others by agreeing to too much, male perfectionists often get caught up in competing in the workplace and in sports.

According to author William Pollack, Ph.D., in his book *Real Boys: Rescuing Our Sons from the Myths of Boyhood*, athletics can become "an arena where boys are pushed to become compulsive about doing well, making themselves strong, or beating the competition." Success in sports can lead to greater success in social relationships, lucrative college scholarships, and even a network for employment. It's no wonder many boys and young men become obsessed with seeking perfection in this area. But that can be dangerous, too. This compulsiveness can lead to training excessively, masking or ignoring serious injuries, or playing overzealously.

Coaches and parents sometimes push young men to pursue impossible standards of perfection on the playing field, asking young athletes to play out their middle-aged fantasies of success. In this case, it's dangerous to be talented because sports can become an all-or-nothing pursuit of winning. Pollack tells the story of one perfectionistic young man, Peter. He'd won his school's MVP awards in both baseball and football, and worked hard to meet his family's expectations for success. "They wanted an academic genius and a stand-out athlete," said Peter, "and I've always tried with all my might to give them what they wanted."

Peter was determined to repeat his MVP performance the following year, but early in the football season, he injured his knee. He continued to play, though, and hid the severity of his pain from his coach and his parents until his knee gave out on the field. He was despondent in the hospital, worried about how his parents would react—not to his painful injury but to the fact that he'd miss the rest of the season. He said, "I haven't looked my mother in the eye since it happened. How could I have done this to her? I ruined her life!" His reaction might seem odd to some, but not to a perfectionist whose perspective might be distorted.

Ever since he could remember, Peter felt pressure to be the family hero. The thought of letting his parents down left him despressed. He couldn't see what others outside the situation did but blamed himself for being weak and unable to compete. He couldn't take pride in his real accomplishments but only saw the goal he couldn't attain.

Many young men who are injured in sports try to do what Peter did: not let others know. And many of them end up with the same results: making the initial injury worse.

For many men, this competitive, "never say die" attitude carries over into the world of work. Males have traditionally been the workaholics in our society, pushing themselves hard to build a stable career and often missing out on the joys of family as they attend one more meeting, repair one more piece of machinery, make yet one more late-night transglobal conference call. Like women, men too can be constrained by gender expectations, trying to be the "perfect" husband and father: the good provider, the steady shoulder to lean. Men learn early to hide their feelings of fear and anxiety and vulnerability.

Just as women can burn themselves out trying to have it all, so can men. Many men realize only later in life that they've been pursuing an impossible dream: That ephemeral point in their careers where they could finally feel totally accomplished and proud never really exists. They wake up one day to discover that they've paid dearly for the compulsive pursuit of perfection at work. It can cost them their relationships with family and friends. But this can be prevented. The trick is learning early on to overcome perfectionism and find balance in life.

If **A** is success in life, then **A** equals **x** plus **y** plus **z**. Work is **x**; **y** is play; and **z** is keeping your mouth shut.

—Albert Einstein

You can take a few lessons on this from the girls and women around you. Perfectionists in general tend to have trouble asking for help, but men especially in our society can feel awkward about reaching out to others. Maybe you can learn how from watching the women in your life reach out to others when they need help. You have the right, just like your sister, to talk to a parent when something is bothering you. You shouldn't be expected to hold your emotions in check and go it alone. It may be really uncomfortable at first, and you may feel you're risking looking foolish or less manly. But with practice, you'll feel more comfortable showing the whole range of emotions inside of you, and others will appreciate knowing the real, caring human being inside.

Perfectionist boys and girls are more alike than different, when it comes right down to it. Both need to learn to admit their vulnerabilities and accept that they will not attain perfection at home, at work, or in their relationships. You have the right to be loved, admired, and respected not just for your accomplishments but who you are as a person. And you have the right to take care of yourself and begin to take responsibility for your own life choices.

Tips for Avoiding Burnout — Now and Later

1. **Learn how to say no.** Give yourself permission to stop doing something you do only to please someone else. Practice saying no in front of the mirror until you can say it without reservation, without hesitation, in an "I mean it" tone of voice. Then use your newly acquired skills at your earliest opportunity.

Lila, fifteen, was amazed at how she felt the first time she said no. "When the editor of our school newspaper moved to another state, the adviser called me to take his place. I knew I already had enough to handle for the rest of the term. So I said no. The next day I got another call asking if I had changed my mind. I said no again. I felt exhilarated and full of energy and power. It was great!"

2. **Learn when to say yes.** Not to more work, not to another competition, but to something personally rewarding. Bake a treat instead of reworking your short story for your creative writing class. Take a chance and go bowling with a group of people just to clown around.

Michael, sixteen, surprised himself when he agreed to watch his niece and nephew one afternoon. He took them to the park, and the three of them had a wonderful time building a miniature city in the sandbox. "I didn't think little kids could be so much fun," Michael said. "They gave me an excuse to just play for a change."

3. **Start prioritizing your activities.** Space them out more efficiently. Make a list of all your activities. Include everything— from after-school lessons to assignment due-dates to dances to weekend jobs and household chores. When you're done, mark your most important activities number 1. Then mark the second-most important activities number 2, and so on. (Use a pencil; you're likely to change your mind a few times.) When you've finished, look closely at the results. If at all possible, start eliminating the lowest priorities and work backwards, erasing as many items as you realistically can. Then enter your activities in a weekly planner or monthly calendar.

Look at the schedule you've created for yourself. Does it seem workable? Have you left at least one or two nights a week for yourself to do whatever you choose whenever you choose to do it. Be spontaneous! Be imaginative! Be silly!

Check It Out !

Making Every Day Count: Daily Readings for Young People on Solving Problems, Setting Goals, and Feeling Good About Yourself by Pamela Espeland and Elizabeth Verdick (Minneapolis: Free Spirit Publishing, 1998). Start each day with a thought-provoking quotation, a brief essay, and positive I-statement.

Smart Girls: A New Psychology of Girls, Women, and Giftedness by Barbara A. Kerr, Ph.D. (Scottsdale, AZ: Gifted Psychology Press, 1997). Describes successful women who started out as gifted girls with perfectionist tendencies.

7

Ways to Gain Control over Your Life

> It's not so much how busy you are, but why you are busy.
> The bee is praised; the mosquito is swatted.
>
> —Marie O'Conner

It's the night before your research paper is due. You're sitting at your desk surrounded by piles of paper, stacks of books, chewed-up pencils, empty soda cans, and potato chip crumbs. You look at your watch . . . midnight. You look at the screen on your computer and gasp. It's blank, as is your mind.

You're in BIG trouble.

Things are OUT OF CONTROL.

How did they reach that point? You knew about this paper a month ago, and somehow you let it slide. And it's not the first time you've found yourself in this fix.

But it could be the last. You can take control of your life—without giving in to your perfectionism. The secret lies in recognizing what you can and can't control.

Theologian Reinhold Niebuhr said it best when he wrote what's become known as the Serenity Prayer:

> God grant me the serenity
> To accept the things I cannot change,
> The courage to change the things I can,
> And the wisdom to know the difference.

There are things you can't change—like the deadline for your research paper. And there are things you can change—like the way you go about trying to meet it.

Tried-and-True Ways to Get Things Done

Anything is easier if you break it down into bite-sized pieces. For example, you've been told to write twenty pages on some aspect of life in the Ice Age. You can think of it as a stack of blank paper crying out to be filled with somewhere around five thousand words (aargh!)—or you can think of it in several manageable steps to be accomplished in a logical order. Like this:

STEP 1. Choose your focus. Is there anything you're particularly interested in—art, religion, family structure, how Ice Age humans built their homes, what they wore, or what they ate? Maybe you can center your paper around that.

Chloe, sixteen, likes to write and read poetry. Asked to write a paper on contemporary life in India, she decided to read some Indian poets in translation. She was able to use their firsthand observations of their culture as the basis of her paper, and she got to do something she enjoys—immerse herself in poetry.

Erik, fifteen, has always been fascinated by bridges. Given an assignment to write about an old European city, he chose Venice—a city of more than four hundred bridges.

STEP 2. Compile a bibliography of resources on your topic. One or two afternoons at the library can yield more sources of information than you'll ever need—especially if you know where to look. *The Reader's Guide to Periodical Literature* is an obvious (and excellent) resource for articles, but don't stop there. Your librarian can point you toward all kinds of reference books and specialized indexes, including CD-ROM directories and encyclopedias. If you have Internet access at home, you might not even have to leave the comfort of your room to perform research. You're only a click away from library catalogs, useful databases, and topic-specific Web sites. Use a search engine like *yahoo.com* or *google.com* and you'll be on your way to many sources and great amounts of information.

STEP 3. Take careful notes on what you read. You can scribble them in a spiral-bound notebook, type them into your laptop, or write them on index cards. Many people find that cards are still the easiest way to organize and reorganize the ideas that start forming as they begin their research. Invest in some 5" x 8" notecards—much roomier than the usual 3" x 5" variety. Use them to jot down memorable paragraphs, sentences, or phrases you encounter along the way. (Be sure to use quotation marks if you're copying exactly, and always remember to note the source of your ideas!)

STEP 4. Write an outline based on your notes. The more detailed the better, because then all you'll have to do is . . .

STEP 5. Fill in the blanks between the items on your outline. In other words, if you complete steps 1 to 4, you'll be well on your way to having that paper done—on time.

Check It Out !

Research Reports: A Guide for Middle and High School Students by Helen Sullivan and Linda Sernoff (Brookfield, CT: Millbrook Press, 1998). The book includes step-by-step instructions to writing a report: selecting a topic, forming an outline, researching information, taking notes, conducting an interview, using quotations and footnotes, writing the draft, revising, using graphics, compiling a bibliography, and producing the final report.

Psychologist Alan Lakein calls this the "Swiss cheese" method. You "punch holes" into big projects by dividing them into smaller and more manageable sections. When you're ready to start writing, you should have punched so many holes into your assignment that it looks like Swiss cheese.

Breaking a project down in this way makes sense. So how are you going to make sure that you actually do it? Try getting permission from your teacher to hand in each part as you complete it. This will give you a push toward finishing the different items on schedule—and it may also give you the benefit of being able to discuss your work-in-progress with your teacher.

If that isn't possible, draw up a contract with yourself. Set a deadline for each part, and then meet it! Build in some rewards for good behavior: going for a bike ride after you finish your research or watching a movie when you're done with your outline.

○ **Ice Age Paper Due Friday February 20!!!**

1. Choose focus by monday February 2.

2. Go to library after school on Wednesday and on Saturday morning.

3. Organize notes by Tuesday February 10.

4. Do outline by Thursday February 12 and talk about it
   ○ with teacher during study hall.

5. Start writing paper on Friday after school. (Movie with Lisa & Tom at 7:00.) Try to get first two pages done.

6. Write AT LEAST another five pages on Saturday.

7. Have paper halfway done by Tuesday February 17.

8. HAND IN on Friday morning!

○ I promise to stick to this schedule—no excuses!

signed:

Once you've signed your contract, stick to it. You'll be surprised at how easy it is to move from step to step. Resist the urge to procrastinate, no matter how strong it is. Ten minutes in front of the TV can turn into three hours; five minutes with a mystery novel can become an all-night page-turner.

> Procrastination is the thief of time.
>
> —Edward Young

What if you get stuck? Really stuck—as in paralyzed, empty-headed, and desperate? You've written ten pages, and you don't like them. Should you tear them up, throw away the scraps, and start over?

Maybe—and maybe not. First, ask yourself why you don't like them. Is it because they aren't perfect? Or do they just need a little cosmetic surgery?

In his book *Mindstorms: Children, Computers, and Powerful Ideas*, Seymour Papert, Ph.D., discusses "debugging" computer software. Like any good metaphor, it translates across several disciplines. Papert explains that someone who is writing a computer program should never ask "Is it right?" or "Is it wrong?" but "Is it fixable?" Few (if any) software programs run flawlessly the first time. Instead of erasing it and starting over, it's far preferable to try to fix it—or "debug" it.

See if you can find the "bugs" in your paper. Or mark the specific sentences or paragraphs that "bug" you the most. Then go to work fixing them, one at a time.

Whether you're writing a paper, preparing a Chopin nocturne for your senior recital, learning your lines for the school play, or training for a marathon, there are always two ways to perceive a task: as a horrible whole or as a series of parts to be completed one after another.

TIP

Do it.
Meet your deadline.
Review it.
Improve it.

Forget about waiting until you can make your assignment "the best ever" (which may mean you never turn it in) and instead concentrate on making something as good as it can be under the circumstances. Watch your time carefully, always move forward, meet project deadlines, and then concern yourself with returning later for possible improvement.

5 Steps to Complete a Project

1. Choose your focus.

2. Gather all the materials you need to get the job done. (Sharp pencils. A piano. Your running shoes. Whatever.)

3. Get organized. Decide what to do first, second, third . . . twenty-third.

4. Divide and conquer. Do one part at a time, take one step at a time, memorize one line at a time, play one note or chord at a time. Then move on to the next, and the next, and the next until—surprise!—you're through.

5. Even if your performance isn't perfect, don't stop until you've completed the first draft, the first run-through, the first read-through. You can always go back later and smooth out the rough spots.

> A man would do nothing if he waited until he
> could do it so well that no one could find fault.
>
> —John Henry Cardinal Newman

Setting Reasonable Standards for Yourself

Your assignment is to write on some aspect of life in the Ice Age. It's not to write a study suitable for publication in a scholarly journal, nor is it to one-up Jean Auel's 425-page novel *The Clan of the Cave Bear.*

You don't always have to be the best and the brightest. Sometimes it's enough do a competent job. That's one of the hardest things for the hard-core perfectionist to learn—especially in a society as competitive as ours.

The need to compete makes people do strange things. Some athletes use illegal steroids to promote muscle growth, risking dangerous side effects later in life. Some students are so determined to be first in every subject that all they do is study—and literally ace themselves out of admission to many colleges, which look for well-rounded students (those with extracurricular activities and a lively social life).

There are many people who didn't come in first, yet came out ahead in the long run. Michelle Kwan, heavily favored to win the gold medal for women's figure skating in the 1998 Olympics, came away with the silver. But she proceeded to win her next nine competitions and the most lucrative product endorsement contracts. Jessie Jackson sought the Democratic nomination twice, in 1984, when he came in third, and in 1988, when he placed second. He still ranks as a highly respected political leader.

E.B. White's wonderful book *Charlotte's Web* didn't win the Newbery Award in 1953, but it's a lot better known than *Secret of the Andes,* which did. Buzz Aldrin wasn't the first man on the moon, but he never complained about following Neil Armstrong down the landing-module ladder into history.

> Being defeated is often a temporary condition.
> Giving up is what makes it permanent.
>
> —Marilyn vos Savant

In any contest, there's only one first place and one last place. In between is a wide middle range, with plenty of room to explore, experiment, and experience your possibilities. Setting too-high standards for yourself prevents you from ever finding this middle range and all the surprises it holds. And it prevents you from learning and growing.

You don't have to do everything right all the time. In fact, it's usually preferable to do things on time—even if it means making compromises with yourself. Faced with the choice between turning in a paper that doesn't completely satisfy you and not turning one in at all, the better choice is always the former.

Planning Positive Alternate Paths

Scientists, inventors, and other creative types know that there's usually more than one solution to a problem. They learn to leave themselves an "out" in case a particular approach leads nowhere or they get bogged down. They become adept at shifting gears, changing directions, and taking positive alternate paths—different ways to go in the event of a dead end or an unforeseen discovery.

- In 1608, Dutch spectacle-maker Hans Lippershey was holding a lens in each hand when he happened to look through both of them at the same time. The result? He invented the telescope.

- In the 1880s, George Washington Carver of the Tuskegee Institute set out to find value in what other people saw as waste. He transformed the peanut, then considered an insignificant crop and "monkey food," into a multibillion dollar industry. Some of the innovative products he derived from the peanut include beverages, pickles, sauces, meal, bleach, wood filler, washing powder, metal polish, paper, ink, plastics, shaving cream, rubbing oil, linoleum, shampoo, axle grease, and synthetic rubber.

- In 1982, Lonnie Johnson was trying to design an environmentally friendly heat pump that used water rather than Freon. When his pump accidentally shot a stream of water across the room, he realized the device would make a great water gun. It took some time, but he converted the pump, and the Super Soaker was delivered to toy stores in 1990—an instant hit.

- In the 1980s, sculptor Patricia Billings faced a professional disaster. A sculpture she had worked on for four months shattered. She went to work developing an additive that would increase the longevity of plaster. After sixteen years of experimenting in her basement, seventy-year-old Patricia invented Geobond, a nontoxic, indestructible, fireproof building material that could revolutionize the construction industry.

Mistakes are the portals of discovery.
—James Joyce

How can you plan positive alternate paths? Here are some suggestions:

1. Make friends with uncertainty and ambiguity. This is very difficult for perfectionists, who are usually so uncomfortable leaving anything to chance that they plan their lives months in advance.

Leave some room for unplanned events—spontaneous discoveries, sudden decisions. If the thought makes you very uneasy, start small. Take a walk one day without planning where you'll go or how long you'll be gone. Just walk, following whatever route interests you even slightly. When you start getting tired, turn around and head back. Then jot down a few of the surprises you saw along the way.

2. Give yourself permission to make mistakes. This is another terrifying prospect for perfectionists, who equate mistakes with abject failure and being "no good."

Some of the best ideas have come out of goofs, bloopers, and outright accidents. Mistakes can be positive learning experiences, if you let yourself learn from them. Many perfectionists deny their mistakes, cover them up, or (even worse) refuse to try anything new for fear of making a mistake. They keep traveling the same old risk-free paths over and over again.

But a mistake can be a wonderful thing. It stimulates your curiosity. ("What went wrong, and where?") It sparks your investigative skills. ("Hmm, let's look at this and dig into that and see if we can find some answers.") It spurs your creative energies. ("I think I'll try this . . . and if it doesn't work, I'll try that.") And it adds to your store of useful experience. ("At least I know not to do it that way again.")

> Mistakes are a fact of life. It is the response to error that counts.
>
> —Nikki Giovanni

3. Be flexible. To plan—and follow—positive alternate paths, you have to be willing to step off the path you're on. And that can be scary.

It can also be exciting. Who knows what you'll discover . . . who knows where you'll end up.

Master chef Julia Child didn't set out to change the way America eats. She was a spy in World War II and the wife of a diplomat when she took her first cooking class at age thirty-seven at Le Cordon Bleu in Paris. She didn't publish her first cookbook until 1961 at the age of forty-nine.

The great American writer James Baldwin started out as a preacher as a teen. He later recounted stories about this time of his life in his 1953 novel *Go Tell It on the Mountain*.

Poet Langston Hughes worked as a steward on a freighter and then as a busboy in a hotel until he put three of his poems next to the plate of American poet Vachel Lindsay. A scholarship to Lincoln University in Pennsylvania followed.

Tom Hanks worked as a bellboy, Denzel Washington as a coffin polisher, Danny DeVito as a hairdresser, Carol Burnett as a hatcheck girl, Jay Leno as a mechanic, David Letterman as a weather announcer, and Dennis Franz as a postal carrier.

4. Give yourself time. You can't always plan positive alternate paths. They sometimes come to you like bolts of lightning—"aha!" experiences that point toward solutions you might not have come up with in a million years.

That's not planning. That's inspiration.

The great inventor Thomas Edison once said, "Genius is one percent inspiration and ninety-nine percent perspiration." What he didn't say is that inspiration isn't necessarily on-call twenty-four hours a day. In other words, you can't just sit down at your desk, grab a pen, and say, "Okay, I'm ready!"

For centuries, artists have personified inspiration and called it the Muse. The Muse has been characterized as a woman-spirit who comes and goes pretty much as she pleases. If you're not ready when she is, you lose!

When you schedule every second of your life, you don't leave room for the Muse. Inspiration often comes in quiet moments—moments when you let your mind wander freely. You may have noticed that some of your best ideas pop into your head just as you're falling asleep at night, when you've finally let go of your hold on your brain. Why not leave space during the day as well?

3M, makers of Post-it Notes and countless other successful products (like Scotch tape), has stressed the importance of giving people time to think. They offered a policy that allowed employees to work on projects of their own choosing for 15 percent of their time. Called "bootlegging," it led to many interesting (and profitable) discoveries and inventions—Post-it Notes being just one.

Try some bootlegging of your own. Set aside half an hour a day—or an hour, or even two—to pursue your own interests, apart from schoolwork or structured extracurriculars. See what happens when the Muse can find you and you've got time to listen.

Or, if you prefer, go looking for her. The Muse tends to hang around art and artists—the evidence of her influence, and the people who heed it. Take a Saturday afternoon to wander around a gallery or a museum. Spend a morning reading poems or short stories. Go to a classical music concert or ballet. Watch a painter or sculptor at work. Page through an art book. See a play.

Can't figure out what to do with that Ice Age paper? Wander through some pictures of the famous painted caves at Lascaux,

France: the antlered deer and wild cattle on the walls the black-and-red horses on the ceiling. Imagine the people who painted them. The caves are pitch-black inside, so they must have carried some sort of light—probably lamps filled with animal fat, with moss for wicks. Imagine the light flickering across the cave walls and how the animals painted there must have looked as if they were moving. Close your eyes and smell the burning fat from the lamps, and feel the soft fur of your bison cloak. . . . Now you're ready to write!

> The most beautiful thing in the world is, precisely, the conjunction of learning and inspiration. Oh, the passion for research and the joy of discovery!
>
> —Wanda Landowska

Getting to Know the Real You

If someone came up to you and said, "Tell me about yourself," how would you answer? With a long description of what you do? Or with a verbal picture of who you are?

People often define themselves by their occupations. Go to any gathering of adults and you'll hear what sound like ritual conversations: "Hello, I'm so-and-so. What do you do?" "I'm a lawyer/baker/teacher/parent/entrepreneur/student"—and so on. We derive our identities from our jobs.

That may be one reason why some people feel lost when they retire; some even become ill. Unless they find new interests and avenues to explore, once they leave their jobs, they lose their sense of themselves and drive their loved ones bonkers.

There's nothing wrong with being proud of what you do, but is that all you are? What about the rest of you? Don't you want people to know more about you than the fact that you're class president, a straight-A student, or captain of the hockey team?

Wouldn't it be nice if, instead of introducing you as "the smartest kid in class" or "the state record-holder in the 100-meter dash" someone introduced you as being humorous, kind, thoughtful, brave, and a good person to have as a friend?

It's hard to break old habits. But the next time someone asks, "What do you do?" try responding in a completely new way. Say,

"I read old science-fiction novels," "I collect antique animal statues," "I stargaze," or "I watch Alfred Hitchcock movies." You're still talking about what you do, but in a different way. By giving people a glimpse into your interests, you're giving them a glimpse into you. And that can lead to some interesting conversations.

Getting to know the real you also means allowing yourself to feel all your emotions. That means experiencing and expressing a wide range of feelings—including "imperfect" ones like anger, guilt, anxiety, aggression, sadness, jealousy, and fear. Many perfectionists grow up believing that they have to be "good boys" and "good girls." They're told not to cry, not to get mad, not to shout, not to feel sorry for themselves, not to complain. "Imperfect" feelings may not fit your image of yourself, but they're there anyway, and you know it. Unless you're from the planet Vulcan, you need to let them out. Keeping them locked inside leads to unhappiness, stress, and even physical and emotional illness.

Find constructive outlets for the feelings you can't talk about. Instead of turning your anger inward, yell, scream, kick a can, or hit something. Just be sure it's something soft. Eighteen-year-old Lucia once got so furious that she hit the steering wheel of her car—and broke her arm.

What happens when you start facing your "imperfect" feelings? You also start realizing that maybe, just maybe, you're slightly imperfect yourself. And that's a positive step toward taking control of your perfectionism—and your life.

It's okay to be imperfect. We live in an imperfect world. Which, as it happens, is lucky for us. Imagine what it would be like to live in a perfect world. No problems, no pain, no challenges, no mysteries, no excitement, no creativity, no risks.

BORINNNNNGGGGGG!

Check It Out !

How to Get Control of Your Time and Your Life by Alan Lakein (New York: New American Library, 1996). Learn how to run your life efficiently by tackling procrastination, scheduling, and problem-solving.

The 7 Habits of Highly Effective Teens: The Ultimate Teenage Success Guide by Sean Covey (New York: Simon & Schuster, 1998). A light approach to tackling serious issues—friendships, peer pressure, self-esteem, parental relationships, coping skills, conflict, and many others.

Mind Tools—Time Management Skills
www.psywww.com/mtsite/page5.html
A wealth of information, including action plans, activity logs, time estimates, and prioritized to-do lists.

Time Management Techniques
caps.unc.edu/TimeMgnt.html
Let the University of North Carolina at Chapel Hill show you how to create a master schedule to help you stay on top of the problem of time management.

8

Learning to Reward Yourself and Savor Success

> There is only one success—to be able to spend your life in your own way.
>
> —Christopher Morley

"Eighth grade was a real turning point in my life," says Daniel, sixteen. "Up until then my father had worked for a large corporation and was a perfectionist: driven and competitive. Suddenly he decided to change things. He quit his job and started his own business.

"Meanwhile I was on the school swim team. I was also a perfectionist: driven and competitive just like my father. One day I hurt my ankle and wasn't able to compete anymore.

"This all happened at around the same time, and it made a BIG change in our family. Everyone loosened up and started doing more things together. Instead of running in different directions, we sat around the dinner table in the evening and talked. We even took vacations together!"

■ ■ ■

"During my first year in college," says Tamika, twenty, "my best friend and roommate died in her sleep. It was a terrible shock. Kelly had a congenital heart defect that no one knew about.

"I spent a lot of time thinking about Kelly and why she'd died and what it all meant. I started realizing how hard it is to plan for tomorrow, since you may not even have a tomorrow. And I started realizing that life is short and precious and you should make the most of it.

"There were things I wanted to do, but I'd been putting them off. I decided not to wait any longer. I started running a mile a day, then two, then three. I learned how to paint with watercolors. I said yes to dates instead of always staying in my room studying. I started having fun!"

■ ■ ■

"My mother's stroke really opened my eyes," says Alicia, seventeen. "She's okay now, but for a while it was scary. She was always such a perfectionist.

After the stroke she had to slow down and take it easy. She started going to counseling, and she's a lot different than she used to be.

"Her stroke forced me to start looking at my own perfectionist tendencies. There are more important things in life than being picky, picky, picky. Now I consciously try to relax more, to not be so hard on myself and other people, and to let things go when I can't change them—or shouldn't bother.

"I used to be proud of being a perfectionist. Now I don't think the stress and pressure are worth it."

■ ■ ■

The decision to be less of a perfectionist is a personal and private one. No one can make it for you. It's something you have to choose for yourself. Daniel, Tamika, and Alicia all did—but only after going through a "conversion" experience as a result of a major life change. Before then, they had just as many perfectionistic tendencies as you probably do!

But you don't have to wait for a crisis or a disaster. Maybe you can make an informed, proactive decision instead of a reactive one. From reading this book, you should have a good sense of what perfectionism can do to your mind, your body, your relationships, and your life. Maybe that's all it will take for you to start letting go.

You can choose to change. In Chapter 5, we talked about ways to ease up on yourself. In Chapter 7, we explored ways to take control of your life. These are all positive actions you can take to make your life less driven, less stressful, and more enjoyable. And maybe you're already trying some of them. In fact, maybe you're hard at work trying to do a perfect job of becoming less perfectionist!

Whoa! Time out! Becoming less perfectionist should not create more ways for you to be hard on yourself, push yourself, and feel bad because you're not doing it all. In fact, an important part of becoming less perfectionist involves feeling good about yourself for who you are. And that involves believing that you deserve to feel good about yourself. And when you believe that, you start treating yourself better.

When was the last time you patted yourself on the back, pampered yourself, or let yourself relax and enjoy life? Maybe it's been so long that you've forgotten how.

Let's do something about that.

Low-Cost (or No-Cost) Rewards to Give Yourself

You may need to practice being good to yourself. Here's a warm-up exercise. You'll need two blank sheets of paper and a pencil or pen.

1. Start by numbering from 1 to 20 down the left-hand side of one sheet of paper. Now list—in the order they occur to you— your major accomplishments. With one restriction: Do *not* list any grades, first places, or best ofs.

What's left? How about accomplishments in your personal relationships? Ideas you've had that made you especially proud? Solutions to problems in your everyday life that you've come up with on your own? Ways you've helped people or let them help you? What about your first jump off the high-dive, or the time you mowed your neighbor's lawn, or the day you passed your driver's test? What about the afternoon you made a loaf of bread from scratch and it wasn't just edible, it was delicious?

2. Number from 1 to 20 down the left-hand side of the other sheet of paper. Now list the events in your life that gave you the most pleasure. Start as far back in time as you like.

Again, no fair including the sixth-grade state spelling bee you won, or your first MVP trophy from the soccer league. Instead, what about the wintry Saturday afternoon when your mom taught you how to play Monopoly? Or the day your dad took you on a walk in the park without the rest of the family? What about the concert you went to last summer? Or the vacation you took with your best friend's family to the Blue Ridge Mountains?

Interestingly, the events we remember most clearly and fondly are often those that didn't take much time or effort. And they probably didn't have much to do with the things we normally devote our energy to pursuing—like getting good grades or beating out the competition.

3. Finally, put your two lists side by side (the better to see them both at once). Choose an item off the first list that you think is worthy of a reward. Then choose something off the second list you'd like to do again as a way of rewarding yourself.

Maybe you can't repeat that vacation—but what about asking your mom for a Monopoly rematch? Or inviting your dad for a walk?

Can you think of brand-new ways to reward yourself? Are there things you've always wanted to do? (Not accomplish—just do.) Like throw a dinner party for your best friends, try your hand at photography, go stargazing at midnight, or listen to *La Bohème?* Make a wish list and add to it whenever something else comes to mind.

Because many perfectionists are inveterate planners, you may need to build your rewards into your schedule, at least until you form the habit of being good to yourself. If you know that Friday is the big biology test, reserve Friday evening for roller-skating. If your clarinet recital is set for Sunday afternoon, plan to celebrate Sunday evening with your family and friends. Remember: You deserve it!

Accepting Praise from Others and Praising Yourself

Many perfectionists downplay their accomplishments. Some fall victim to the "impostor syndrome." They seem to sail effortlessly from one achievement to another, but deep down inside they feel like fakes, like frauds, and they live in constant fear of getting caught. They attribute their success to luck, good timing, or some other factor out of their control. They can't accept praise because they honestly don't feel they deserve it. They wave it aside or change the subject.

Do any of these confessions sound familiar to you?

> Whenever I aced a math quiz, I thought it was because I had just happened to study the right homework problems the night before. I was sure that if I had studied other problems, I would have failed. It took a long time to admit to myself that I was actually good at math.
> —Melanie, 14

> My teachers liked me a lot, but I could never really trust them. I was afraid that one day they would see the real me—the unlikeable person I thought I was.
> —Steven, 12

> When I was made first-chair violin in our school orchestra, I thought it was all over—that the conductor would finally discover I couldn't really play and had been bluffing all along. It wasn't until the next year, when I made first chair again, that I started thinking that maybe I had talent!
> —Alisha, 17

Do you make excuses for your ability? Do you get uncomfortable when people praise you? Does it sometimes seem as though you're hiding behind a facade, a bogus you that only looks good?

The next time someone offers you a compliment, try this: Open your mouth and say "Thank you." Not "Thank you, but…" Just "Thank you." It will be all over before you know it. It's a lot easier than you think!

Refusing to accept a compliment is like refusing to accept a gift, and that insults the giver. Even if you don't think you deserve to be praised—even if you feel like an impostor—you can still be polite and gracious. After a while, you may start believing your ears. And you may actually start enjoying it when people say wonderful things about you to your face.

> You can tell the character of every man when you see how he receives praise.
>
> —Seneca

You should feel terrific when someone says "Good job!" or "You look great today!" or "Congratulations!" We all need the approval of others. And they need our approval, too. If you're the overly critical type (another perfectionist trait), try substituting nice words for "helpful suggestions." Your mom may go into shock the first time you give her a compliment, especially if you haven't done it for years, but you'll both feel better for it.

What about praising yourself? Many perfectionists find this especially hard to do. No matter how well they do something, they're convinced that it's still not good enough. Their standards are so high that they can't possibly meet them.

Try this simple exercise in self-praise. Go to a mirror and say, "I'm okay." It may feel weird at first, but keep doing it until you start believing it. You'll come away with renewed self-confidence and a more positive self-image.

Savoring Your Success

It's your first time ever on skis. You stand there feeling foolish while babies barely out of diapers whiz past on both sides. Your parents are patient, but you wish you were anywhere else.

Deep breath . . . bend those knees . . . grasp those poles . . . take that first hesitant sliding step . . . and you're off! An hour later you're unbuckling your skis, red-faced and panting and proud of yourself. You fell down countless times, but you did it!

Or it's your first time ever in front of a large audience. You're the magician in the annual school talent show, and now you're wishing you could make yourself disappear.

Deep breath . . . stand up straight . . . reach into hat . . . and pull out rabbit. Everyone applauds! The rest of the show sails by without a hitch—even the part where you saw your history teacher in half. You're a hit!

Take time—make time—to savor your successes. Perfectionists have a habit of doing one thing after another without ever pausing to feel good about what they just accomplished. Put your feet up, relax, and go over the details in your mind. Focus on your triumphs and ignore your mistakes.

Do you have trouble relaxing? That's another common characteristic among perfectionists. They're so busy trying to do everything right that they can't slow down long enough to take it easy.

The inability to relax has become such a problem in our culture that hospitals and clinics offer stress-reduction programs aimed at helping people to loosen up. Before you go that far, here are things you can try at home.

Meditation. If you want to know more about this tried-and-true rejuvenator, read about it at the library. Or ask around among your friends or their parents. There are many different kinds of meditation: Zen, transcendental, and tai chi chuan (which combines slow, graceful physical movements with meditation). Maybe one is right for you.

Meditation works. Your heartbeat and metabolism slow. Your oxygen consumption goes down. And you emerge refreshed and alert. Meditation can alleviate stress, allowing people more calm and increased inner strength as they sort out the stressors in their lives. Many people who meditate feel that the deep rest and relaxation experienced by the body and the central nervous system during meditation can improve overall health.

Listening to soothing music. Using music to relax has become increasingly popular in our stressed-out society. Natural sounds (wind blowing through trees, waves rolling in, birds or whales singing), soft classical music, modern synthesized music, smooth jazz—all these types can be relaxing. Start with one or more of these; you'll soon make "finds" of your own.

- *Solitudes.* Each CD in this series contains a full hour of therapeutic sounds—canoe paddles dipping into water, falling rain, crickets on a country night.
- Individual artists including Kitaro *(Silk Road),* Paul Winter *(Whales Alive),* George Winston *(December, Autumn),* and Andreas Vollenweider *(Kryptos, Behind the Gardens).*

Yoga. By breathing, stretching, and moving slowly into time-honored positions, you not only can calm down but get into shape. You may find a class at your local community college, park district, or Y. Or go to your bookstore and pick up a copy of *Integral Yoga Hatha* by Sri Swami Satchidananda (Buckingham, VA: Integral Yoga Distribution, 1998), a clear introduction to basic yoga techniques, with lots of illustrations.

Cooking. Fix a pan of fudge, chop a pound of veggies and make homemade soup, knead bread dough, fill the kitchen with delicious aromas. Many people find that cooking relaxes them. There's something about the simple chores of peeling potatoes, measuring flour, and stirring a pan on the stove that gets your mind off your troubles. Cooking lets you use all your senses to create a snack or a meal to share with the people you care about.

Walking. Stroll around the block, or ask a friend to accompany you through a park or the woods. Go at a leisurely pace, giving yourself a chance to notice the things around you—the smells of fresh-cut grass, the sounds of children playing in a park, the colors of new or changing leaves.

Yes, relaxing takes time, but it's time well spent. You think more clearly, your body works better, and you have more energy. Try to make it part of your daily routine and you'll immediately feel the difference.

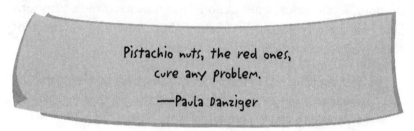

> Pistachio nuts, the red ones,
> cure any problem.
>
> —Paula Danziger

Reading for pleasure. What a luxury it is to read what you want to read, instead of plowing through assignments! Many perfectionists don't leave time for this all-important pursuit. Remember how it felt when you were a child and sat up in bed reading, or curled up on a blanket under a tree, or hid in a closet with a flashlight? Those days don't have to be over.

Aren't you about due to reread *The Lord of the Rings?* Or maybe you miss Madeleine L'Engle's *A Wrinkle in Time.* Or maybe you've been meaning to read *Anna Karenina* or *Their Eyes Were Watching God* or *The Decline and Fall of the Roman Empire* or Sandburg's biography of Lincoln or that new collection of short stories you've been eyeing at your local bookstore or the newest bestseller. . . .

Reading can be your reward and your relaxation all in one. Most kids are avid readers, so it's no secret to you what pleasures books hold. And no matter how much you read, there's always something you haven't read, waiting like buried treasure to be discovered.

If you won't let yourself do pure leisure reading, how about reading books that can help you work through a particular problem? If perfectionism is a problem in your life, you may want to try one or more of the novels described on pages 103–104.

Don't worry if any of them seem too young for you; all that means is they'll take less time to read (and probably have pictures, which always make books more interesting).

> Reading is to the mind what exercise is to the body.
>
> —Sir Richard Steele

Perfectionists may be good at a lot of things, but they're usually not very good at rewarding themselves and savoring their success. In the midst of trying to be the best, they forget to enjoy just being themselves.

How can you tell when it's time to cut back on your busy schedule, relax, and take it easy for a while? One young woman offered these wise words: "It's time to slow down when you get so obsessed that you forget the people in your life, your faith, and your hobbies."

Check It Out !

Be a Perfect Person in Just Three Days! by Stephen Manes (Boston: Houghton Mifflin, 1996). Milo, who wants to be perfect, finds a book by Dr. K. Pinkerton Silverfish that promises to teach him how. He follows all of its instructions to the letter—right down to wearing a broccoli necklace. Read the book and find out why!

Here's to You, Rachel Robinson by Judy Blume (New York: Yearling, 1995). A straight-A high-achieving student, Rachel feels pressured at school by all her activities. People keep pushing her to do more—play the flute, star in the play, run for class president, take accelerated classes at a local college. And then her older brother, Charles, is expelled from boarding school, fanning the flames of trouble at home as well.

On the Devil's Court by Carl Deuker (Boston: Little Brown and Company, 1991). Seventeen-year-old high-school senior Joe Faust dreams of having his best-ever basketball year. Instead, he's headed for his very worst until, in desperation, he strikes a bargain that changes the course of events. Joe is willing to do anything to be the best. "The Great Professor Joseph Faust Senior doesn't understand a son who isn't perfect like he is," says Joe of his father. "If I get a C+ on my report card, you'd think I murdered a nun."

Ordinary Jack by Helen Cresswell (New York: Macmillan Publishing Company, 1977). Jack is the only "ordinary" member of the Bagthorpe family, a clan who show incredible excellence in virtually everything they do. Jack desperately tries to find something that will make him special. Is it possible that becoming a prophet could accomplish this?

Winners and Losers by Stephen Hoffius (New York: Simon & Schuster, 1993). Curt is flabbergasted when his best friend and fellow runner, Daryl Wagner, collapses during a track meet. Diagnosed with a weak heart, Daryl is forced off the team for a time while Curt continues to be coached by Daryl's father. Showing rapid improvement, Curt earns the team's top running spot. When Daryl returns to the squad, the two boys fight to be number one. In the end, winning comes at an unspeakable price.

The Worldwide Online Meditation Center
www.meditationcenter.com
Information on meditation-related terms, relaxation and stress reduction, centering, and healing.

How to Get Others to Ease Up on You

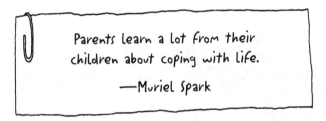

Parents learn a lot from their
children about coping with life.

—Muriel Spark

If your parents are human, they've probably said, "We only want what's best for you." The trouble is, what they often mean is "We only want you to be the best." There's a BIG difference, but even the smartest, nicest, most with-it parents can't see it sometimes.

Loving encouragement sometimes turns into pressure. "We know you can do a good job on that test" becomes "We expect you to get an A." Or "Try your hardest to win the race" becomes "We know you can come in first." Or "We think you should go to college" becomes "We want you to apply to Yale and Harvard and Stanford and get a law degree."

One woman used to cry whenever her son didn't win an essay contest. And her son would think, "I have to win or my mother will cry and it will be all my fault." Another mother used to punish her daughter when she didn't win a dance competition. Naturally the daughter grew to hate dance and eventually quit; she seldom performed well because she was terrified of what would happen if she didn't win.

One father, upset because his son didn't take first place in a piano contest, stormed up to a judge and said, "I want to know what else my son can go into since he didn't win." The judge replied, "He can go into a library and read a book, or he can go into your yard and mow the lawn, or he can go into his room and draw a picture." The father walked away angry, but the judge was right: The boy had many options, and his life wasn't over just because he hadn't won *that* competition on *that* day.

Parents Can Say the Dumbest Things...

When I make a mistake or don't do something right the first time, my mom always says, "What's wrong with you? I thought you were supposed to be gifted."
—Nathan, 15

My father introduces me as "My son, The Brain."
—Sam, 12

Whenever I get straight A's, my parents act like it's no big deal. But when I get a B, it's always, "What happened here? Don't you pay attention in class? What's wrong with you?"
—Courtney, 16

My father redid my whole science project. When I told him I was supposed to do it myself, he said, "I'm just making you look better."
—Talia, 15

The messages parents and other important adults give young people are important. Studies report fascinating—and revealing—differences between the messages heard by perfectionists and their nonperfectionist peers.

Perfectionist students often report being told things like "A job worth doing is worth doing well." "Always finish what you start." "Be number one." "You will be valedictorian someday."

"We want you to get all A's." "If you get any grade but an A, make sure it's an A+."

Nonperfectionist students grow up hearing different messages: "Just do the best you can." "You win some, you lose some." "Better luck next time." "What's done is done." "Live for today and don't worry about tomorrow."

The parents of the most perfectionist students tend to have overly high expectations of them. The parents of the least perfectionist students seem to be more relaxed and accepting. This does not mean that high expectations are harmful. In fact, children achieve more when they and important adults in their lives have high expectations for them—they may enjoy the healthy pursuit of excellence. But expectations that are unrealistic or too high can lead to the distress and anxiety of perfectionism.

Some parents try to relive their own lives through their children's accomplishments. They see their children as giving them a second chance to do all the things they never got around to when they were younger. They sign their children up for piano lessons and insist they continue because they always wanted to study music, or they insist that their kids apply to certain colleges because they always wanted to go there.

Similarly, parents don't want their children to make the same mistakes they made when they were younger. There's nothing wrong with that. It's natural to want to protect someone you love from getting hurt. But remember, mistakes lead the way toward learning. Parents who protect their children too much are depriving them of the opportunity to learn from their mistakes. They teach their children that errors are unacceptable, and that it's more important to succeed than to enjoy and learn from an experience.

Does any of this sound familiar to you? What can you do if your parents are a pain?

Plan Your Strategy

With planning and persistence, you can open the doors to better communication with your parents and other adults in your life.

STEP 1. Decide to talk to your parents. Naming a problem is the first step in solving it, so your initial goal might be to start letting your parents know how you feel. They might not realize there's a problem.

"You must be crazy," one young woman said at the thought. "Mom will hit the roof if I ask her to ease up on me. She'll think I'm just making excuses for not being first and best in everything I do."

Talking to your parents about your uncomfortable feelings might be one of the scariest things you've ever done. It takes courage to risk reaching out like that, even to people who care about you. It means admitting first to yourself, and then to someone else, that you're not perfect. That you *can't* be perfect.

Your parents may seem dense sometimes, but they're not stupid. They really do care about you, even though it might be hard for you to recognize at times. And because they care about you, they'll probably be willing to listen if you approach them respectfully and say, "Mom, Dad, can we talk?"

STEP 2. Choose a good time to talk. Find a time when your parents seem to be in a receptive mood—not distracted by work, not rushing to get somewhere, and not when any of you is angry, agitated, or frustrated. Maybe after dinner one evening when you're all cleaning the kitchen. Or on the weekend after returning from services. Or after you've done something you and they are proud of.

Many parents don't realize that perfectionism can be harmful. They think that all the late nights and stress are normal, natural, and necessary parts of making the grade. And they might never realize how you are feeling if you don't tell them. Remember, there's a good chance your parents are perfectionists, too. If their own lifestyle is hectic and pressured, they might think that everyone who wants to succeed has to live that way. But you don't.

STEP 3. Plan what to say next. So, you've got their attention. How do you begin? Here are three good ways to start a conversation:

- "Mom, Dad, I have a problem that maybe you can help me with. Do you ever feel . . ." And fill in the blank with how you are feeling: that nothing you do ever quite measures up? that you're working too hard to really enjoy and appreciate all the good things in your life, like your family and friends? that if you don't win the election for class president your life will be over?

- "I love you and I want you to be proud of me. Would you still love me if I . . ." Fill in the blank: didn't win this year's MVP award? stopped going to karate lessons before getting my blackbelt? spent my first year of college in town instead of going to a prestigious school halfway across the country?

- "I've been reading this book called *Perfectionism* and took this quiz on pages 2–3. Here's what I found out." Share your answers, and ask them how they'd answer for themselves.

STEP 4. Use I-messages. No matter how you begin, you'll probably be more effective if you focus on using I-messages as you talk.

Focus on your feelings and reactions, not your parents', and you're likely to get better results. Here's a simple structure you can use:

I feel _____

when _____

*because*_____

"I feel anxious when you tell Grandma and Aunt Lulu that I'm going to Harvard because I haven't even applied yet and everyone will think I'm a failure if I don't go." "I feel exhausted when I can't sleep at night because I'm too worried about not getting an A on the next math test." "I feel lonely when I can't ever hang out at the mall with friends on Saturday afternoons because I meet my cello tutor and voice coach then."

Tell your parents how perfectionism is affecting your mind, your body, and your relationships. Be prepared with a few examples: "I have a stomachache and itchy palms for days before grades come out. Even though I know I've worked hard and done my best, I'm so afraid of disappointing you." "My friends have been avoiding me lately. I think it might be because I'm too critical. Am I too critical around home, too?"

CAUTION: Your parents may not be willing to discuss perfectionism with you or do anything else suggested here. They may resent any efforts you make to communicate with them about perfectionism. They may refuse to recognize their own perfectionist tendencies, their too-high expectations of you, or the need to change their behavior toward you in any way.

Or your parents may listen but not do much to really change. Remember, they've been like they are now for a long time, and just because they're adults, just because they understand the concept, that doesn't mean they'll be able to change immediately. You may need to remind them how you feel.

This doesn't mean that you can't continue to help yourself. No matter how your parents respond, you can keep working on your own perfectionist tendencies. You can talk to other adults—teachers, counselors, coaches, or religious leaders. You may need to continue on your own, but you already do a lot of things independently; why not this, too? Take steps to ease up on yourself.

STEP 5. Be prepared with suggestions on how your parents can help, but be ready to compromise. Easing up on you is not the same as letting you have your own way in everything. Don't expect your parents will relax all of their expectations. (Would you really want them to?) Instead, talk about what's bothering you the most.

For example, let's say your parents have always planned your class schedule for you and told you which courses to take. They want you to take all the advanced placement courses your school offers. Maybe there are some classes you want to take just for fun or because they interest you. Ask your parents to help you decide on the best time to fit them in. Remind them of the benefits of exploring many interests when you're young. Would it help to get your school guidance counselor involved?

Or let's say you've been delivering straight A's pretty steadily—at the expense of your social life. Your parents probably aren't about to let you go out every night of the week, but what about one night, or two?

Try to find other areas where you can all practice some give-and-take. The point is to arrive at a happy medium between their goals for you and your goals for yourself.

REMINDER: Stay calm. Any conversation you have with your parents will go much more smoothly if you can keep your temper. Maybe you're angry at them for criticizing the B you got in biology, and maybe you have a right to be angry. You may also be anxious or frustrated or nervous. It's hard talking about our fears and sharing parts of ourselves we feel unsure about, and sometimes our strong emotions can make it even harder. But instead of stomping and screaming and slamming doors, or walking away, try simply telling them how you feel. Let them know that you need their love and support. Chances are you'll get it.

If you really can't talk to your parents, how about writing them a letter? Putting your thoughts and feelings down on paper might be a good way for you to plan what you want to say. Or if you really can't face them in person, it can help you break the ice on the topic. One tip some kids follow is to write a research paper on perfectionism or procrastination and let their parents read it.

Going Public

Once you've planned your course of action and spoken with your parents, it may become easier to talk to the rest of the world—including the teachers, friends, and peers who put pressure on you to be perfect.

> Living up to being labeled gifted can be a problem in school. I wish teachers would realize that just because you're gifted doesn't mean you're smart in every subject.
>
> —Charles, 14

> My geometry teacher knows I get straight A's in all my other courses. He's always saying things like, "I know you can do better in this class. I don't think you're trying hard enough."
>
> —Kimberley, 15

For many kids, problems starts with an older brother or sister who seems to do everything right. You know the story: A kid walks into a class and the teacher says, "You're Jamal Washington? I knew your brother Nico; he was the best student I ever had." Who can live up to that? Who even wants to try?

Like parents, teachers have expectations. Like parents, they can sometimes say dumb things. Like parents, they're worth talking to. Give it a try. It's okay to say, "Ms. Murkle, I feel discounted when you compare me to my sister." Or "Mr. Mupple, I appreciate that you recognize my work, but I feel embarrassed when you repeatedly hold me up as a good example to the rest of the class."

If your friends hang around with you just because you're class president or captain of the basketball team or a straight-A student, maybe you should make new friends. Suzie, sixteen, remembers the first (and last) time she went out with a boy from her philosophy class. She enjoyed herself right up to the moment he walked her to her door and asked to copy her class notes.

People can have mixed feelings about bright, super-achieving classmates. They may admire them on the one hand and be extremely jealous on the other. They may see you as a one-dimensional person: a brain, a jock, the science guy. They may send mixed messages that are difficult to decipher.

The other kids in my class put me down for being smart. They call me "Einstein" and act shocked if I don't get the highest score on a test.

—Jason, 14

My best friend and I are at the top of our class. We like each other a lot, but it seems like we're always competing with each other.

—Erin, 13

My friends resent me for being smart. Sometimes I deliberately answer test questions wrong so I'll get a lower grade and be more like them.

—Timothy, 15

If some of your friends are also perfectionists, consider forming a support group. Start with a few ground rules, including "no competition allowed." Use this group as a place to laugh at your mistakes, talk about your problems with perfectionism, share your procrastination stories, and encourage one another in the healthy pursuit of excellence.

> The closest to perfection a person ever comes is when he fills out a job application form.
>
> —Stanley Randall

Check It Out !

Bringing Up Parents: The Teenager's Handbook by Alex Packer, Ph.D. (Minneapolis: Free Spirit Publishing, 1992). For the inside scoop on communication, mutual respect, and common sense.

Feeling Good: The New Mood Therapy by David D. Burns, M.D. (New York: Avon, 1999). See especially Chapter 14 in this classic adult self-help book.

The Gifted Kids' Survival Guide: A Teen Handbook by Judy Galbraith, M.A., and Jim Delisle, Ph.D. (Minneapolis: Free Spirit Publishing, 1996). Lots of tips on talking to parents, expectations, perfectionism, assertiveness, and more.

10

When and How to Get Help Coping

> Striving for perfection is the greatest stopper
> there is. You'll be afraid you can't achieve it. . . .
> It's your excuse to yourself for not doing anything.
> Instead strive for excellence, doing your best.
>
> —Sir Laurence Olivier

When French historian Alexis de Tocqueville visited the United States in 1835, he observed that Americans "all have a lively faith in the perfectability of man." More than 160 years later, it's still true. As a culture, we're eternally in search of the perfect mate, the perfect job, the perfect body, the perfect family. No wonder your parents keep hoping for you to be the perfect child. No wonder you keep trying to be that perfect child—and perfect student, perfect friend, etc.

The fact is, there's simply no way to achieve perfection.

In 1841, a man named John Humphrey Noyes established a religious community called the Perfectionists. Six years later, in 1847, they formed a colony in Oneida, New York. Noyes taught that anyone who converted to Perfectionism would be free from sin. The people in his community even tried breeding human beings to get perfect children. In 1879, the colony was abandoned—because it was "imperfect." Today all that's left of Noyes's plan is the Oneida company, which manufactures silver plate and stainless steel flatware. It's nice, but it's not perfect.

Countless other religious groups have tried for perfection and failed. Philosophers, artists, and scientists have tried it and failed. Adolf Hitler and the Third Reich tried it and failed.

It never works. It can't work. Forget it! Instead, focus on being yourself, on being human. That's a big enough job all by itself.

> We expect more of ourselves
> than we have any right to.
>
> —Oliver Wendell Holmes Jr.

If you need help coping, it's available. But the first thing you have to do is ask. Talk to a parent, your school counselor, or your minister, priest, or rabbi. Talk to your teachers. Talk to your friends. Surround yourself with people who will hear you out, give you good advice, support you, and appreciate you for who you are, not who they think you should be.

If you think you need professional help, there are counselors who specialize in working with perfectionists. Many communities have mental health centers, some with walk-in counseling. It takes brains and courage to realize when you can't go it alone. The smart people are those who admit it and do something about it. The ones who hold it inside, keep it a secret, and go it alone get deeper into trouble.

How to Tell When It's Time to Get Help

If you have perfectionist tendencies, chances are you'll always have them. Again, having high expectations of yourself and striving to do your best work are positive qualities. But problems arise when you carry your perfectionistic tendencies too far.

How can you tell when you've crossed that line? Go back and reread pages 4–7. Understanding the differences between pursuing excellence and perfection is key to knowing which side of the line you're on.

Generally speaking, people who pursue excellence enjoy the things they do. When they finish a project, they pat themselves on the back and reward themselves. They take honest pride in their work and learn from their mistakes. They're committed but not obsessive, dedicated but not desperate. They know how to relax and have a good time.

Perfectionists, on the other hand, always aim higher than they can reach. They don't know how to enjoy their work or take pride in their accomplishments. When they finish a project, they torture themselves with *if onlys* and *should haves*: "If only I had done it this way." "I should have taken more time." "If only I had done one more thing." "I should have done something else." They stay trapped in the "failure gap" between what is and what might have been.

Perfectionists are never satisfied with living in the present. They're always looking back with regret—or forward with apprehension and fear. For them, the future holds only gloom and doom: "I wonder what terrible thing will happen to me next." They feel as if fate has given them a bad hand of cards and may perceive other people, and the world in general, as out to get them.

One way to distinguish between the pursuit of excellence and perfectionism is by listening to your self-talk. People who pursue excellence use positive self-talk: "Hey, I did a pretty good job." "I'm really proud of myself." "I enjoyed working on that project." "Maybe I didn't take first place, but I tried my hardest, and I feel good about that." Perfectionists use negative self-talk: "Why can't I ever do anything right?" "Look at those two questions I missed." "I just know I'm going to fail." "People are going to figure out that I'm a fake."

While a little bit of negative self-talk is okay, a lot is not. If you're always hard on yourself, you need to find out why. Is it an old, bad habit? Or has something happened recently to make you feel more than usually down and depressed? If you can't sort it out yourself, get help. Go to your parents, a teacher, your school counselor, your minister or priest or rabbi.

Pursuers of excellence can experience periods of perfectionism—times when the going is especially rough, or they have a major setback or failure and slip into negative thought patterns. These periods are no cause for alarm, unless they last longer than a day or two. If you feel as if you've fallen into an emotional hole you can't climb out of, get help. If you need help right away, turn to page 121 and call one of the numbers listed there.

Perfectionism and Teenage Suicide

According to a 1996 Centers for Disease Control (CDC) survey of students in grades 9–12, during the twelve months preceding the survey:

- **24.1** percent had thought seriously about attempting suicide.

- **17.7** percent had made a specific plan to attempt suicide.

- **8.7** percent had attempted suicide.

- **2.8** percent had made a suicide attempt which resulted in an injury, poisoning, or overdose that required medical attention.

Female students (30.4 percent) were much more likely than male students (18.3 percent) to have thought seriously about attempting suicide. Female students (21.3 percent) were much more likely than male students (14.4 percent) to have made a specific plan to attempt suicide, and female students (11.9 percent) were much more likely than male students (5.6 percent) to have actually attempted suicide.

It is easy to see the seriousness and widespread nature of teen suicide. According to the CDC, suicide ranks as the fifth leading cause of death among five- to fourteen-year-olds and the third leading cause for those between fifteen and twenty-four. The sad fact is, every year, five to six thousand teens kill themselves, an average of more than one every ninety minutes.

Why do kids kill themselves? There are many reasons, and perfectionism is among them. Obviously, not all teenage suicides are related to perfectionism—but it's almost certain that some of them are.

It takes courage to live. It take courage to be human. It takes courage to make mistakes, admit them, and even laugh at them. It takes courage to be imperfect—especially in a culture as competitive as ours.

Suicide isn't unique to any one race, class, or IQ level. But people with above-average intelligence seem more prone to it than others. They may have these characteristics as well:

1. They have extremely high expectations of themselves or other people.

2. They form extremely intense relationships.

3. They have a hard time accepting the fact that failure and loss are normal parts of living and being human.

Which group is most likely to have all of these traits? Gifted teens—particularly gifted perfectionist teens.

22 Signs of a Teen in Trouble

Experts have found that teens at risk for depression or becoming suicidal show danger signs in advance. If you notice any of these signs in yourself, talk to an adult. If you notice any of them in a friend, tell an adult you trust.

■ Sudden changes in personality

■ Sudden changes in eating or sleeping habits

- Sudden changes in behavior
- Alcohol or other drug use
- Lack of interest in or withdrawal from planned activities (sports, clubs, social events, etc.)
- Persistent boredom
- Severe depression that lasts a week or longer
- Withdrawal from family and friends; self-imposed isolation
- Inability to have fun
- Concealed or direct suicide threats ★
- Loss of interest in personal grooming
- An illness that has no apparent physical cause
- Preoccupation with death and death-related themes
- Giving away prized possessions to family and friends
- Saying good-bye to family and friends
- Difficulty concentrating
- An unexplained decline in the quality of schoolwork
- A recent suicide of a friend or relative
- A previous suicide attempt
- Talking about suicide, either jokingly or seriously
- Running away from home, family, school, etc.
- Feelings of meaninglessness in life

Remember that you always have options. You can correct mistakes. You can change your mind. You can switch directions from a dead-end road to a positive alternate path. You can rack

---

★ Talk to a trusted adult *right away*. You can also call a Crisis Hotline or Suicide Hotline listed in your yellow pages.

up failures and still be a success. (Like the "Ten Famous People Who Made It Big Despite a Rocky Start" from Chapter 5.) The only time you don't have options is when you're not around to exercise them.

No problem is so overwhelming that suicide is the only solution. If you feel you need more information about suicide right away, you can contact any of the following:

Look under **Suicide Prevention** in your local phone book. Most cities and many towns have suicide prevention hotlines, staffed twenty-four hours a day with people ready and willing to listen.

American Association of Suicidology
4201 Connecticut Avenue NW, Suite 408
Washington, DC 20008
(202) 237-2280
www.suicidology.org
This national clearinghouse is open during business hours (Monday through Friday, 9–5 EST) and can refer you to the crisis center nearest you. Other worthwhile information is included at their Web site.

National Hopeline Network
Kristin Brooks Hope Center
609 East Main Street, Unit 112
Purcellville, VA 20132
1-800-SUICIDE (1-800-784-2433)
www.hopeline.com
This toll-free national crisis hotline serves suicidal or troubled youths. The Web site offers a wealth of constructive information on suicide.

Many schools, concerned with the rising teen suicide rate, are bringing this sensitive topic into their curriculum. You may want to talk to a teacher about the possibility of a special class or discussion session.

Finally: Suicidal thoughts cross almost everyone's mind from time to time. It's not unusual to "flash" on it when you're in the depths of depression or despair.

Even people who seem to have it all—fame, money, and success—have considered suicide. When Billy Joel found himself thinking about it, he wrote the song "You're Only Human," made a record, and donated the money from the sales to the National Center on Youth Suicide Prevention.

> To affirm life is to deepen,
> to make more inward,
> and to exalt the will to live.
>
> —Albert Schweitzer

Failure + Flexibility = Fantastic!

If you have read this book all the way through from the first page to these words, then you already know how normal it is to fail and how necessary it is to be flexible—in setting your goals, in adapting to change, in planning alternate paths.

It's the combination of these two—failure and flexibility—that seems to yield the most fantastic results where human achievement is concerned.

Almost everybody who's made it big failed, flopped, flunked, and goofed many times during their lives. But they turned their failures into successes. (Practice may not make perfect, but enough of it—even practice at failing!—makes possibilities.)

Successful people are those who can blow it and bounce back. They don't sit there feeling sorry for themselves. They get up, dust themselves off, and head in another direction—and keep doing it until they end up where they want to go.

If you could look back at your life and remember every minute, you'd find many failures you've since forgotten. And some of them would surprise you.

What happened the first time you tried to walk? You fell down. The first time you tried to ride a bike? You ran into a tree or skidded off a curve. The first time you tried to hit a baseball with a bat? It whizzed by your nose and you swung at the air. The first time you tried to swim? You splashed and sloshed like a sorry fish.

In fact, any life is a series of failures, an assortment of mistakes, a collection of blunders and missteps. If you've been worrying about failure—stop. Instead, think about what you'd be missing if you never took chances, never took risks, never took that first step toward an uncertain conclusion. Think about what life would be like if you really were perfect. Then be glad you're not!

Check It Out !

No One Saw My Pain: Why Teens Kill Themselves by Andrew E. Slaby, M.D. (New York: W. W. Norton & Company, 1996). A psychiatrist who specializes in depression and crisis intervention profiles cases of suicide and attempted suicide to get at the core of what causes this extreme behavior.

When Living Hurts by Sol Gordon, Ph.D. (New York: Dell, 1994). Alerts readers to the early warning signals of trouble, tells where to seek help, and discusses how to deal with frustration, sadness, and anxiety.

When Nothing Matters Anymore: A Survival Guide for Depressed Teens by Bev Cobain (Minneapolis: Free Spirit Publishing, 1998). A guide to understanding and coping with depression, how and why the condition begins, how it may be linked to substance abuse or suicide, and how to get help.

Psych Central
www.psychcentral.com/resources
Extensive links compiled by an accomplished mental health physician.

SAVE (Suicide Awareness Voices of Education)
www.save.org
Warning signs of suicide, support for suicide survivors, and more.

Index

A

Abdul, Paula, 40
Achievement, 9–11, 18–22
Activities, structured, 9–10
Activity priorities, 77
Adderholdt, Miriam, 63, 66, 129
Addictive, work as, 12–13
Alcott, Louisa May, 58
Aldrin, Buzz, 85
All Grown Up and No Place to Go: Teenagers in Crisis (Elkind), 15
All-or-nothing thinking, 21, 39
Alternative paths, planning positive, 85–90
Ambiguity, 87
American Anorexia/Bulimia Association, 37
American Association of Suicidology, 121
American Psychological Association (APA), 41
Amphetamines, 33–34
ANAD (National Association of Anorexia Nervosa and Associated Disorders), 40
Anorexia, 36, 37–38
APA (American Psychological Association), 41
Approval, need for, 29
Armstrong, Neil, 85
The Artist Formerly Known as Prince, 57
A's, straight, 17–18
Athletics, 5, 38–39, 73–74
Attractiveness, perfect partner, 49

B

Balance in life, 5, 32, 74, 76–77
Baldwin, James, 88
Ball, Lucille, 70
Be a Perfect Person in Just Three Days (Manes), 103
The Beauty Trap (Landau), 15
Benardot, Dan, 38–39
Benson, Peter L., 56
Billings, Patricia, 86
Bingeing and purging. *See* Bulimia
Birth order, 8–9
Birth Order Home Page (Web site), 15
Bliss, Edwin, 16
Blume, Judy, 103
Bode, Janet, 43

Body-image, 38, 39
Brains, perfect partner, 48
A Bright Red Scream (Strong), 41, 42
Bringing Up Parents: The Teenager's Handbook (Packer), 114
Bulimia, 36, 37–38, 41–42
Burnett, Carol, 88
Burnout, 74, 76–77
Burns, David D., 3, 114

C

Caffeine, 32–34
Camp Fire USA (Web site), 56
Carlson, Richard, 56, 67
Carver, George Washington, 86
Cat nap, to stay awake, 36
CDC (Centers for Disease Control), 118–119
Centers for Disease Control (CDC), 118–119
Chadwick, Florence, 58
Character Counts! (Web site), 56
Charlotte's Web (White), 84
Check It Out!, 15, 29, 42–43, 56, 77, 80, 103–104, 114
Child, Julia, 88
Child Trends, Inc. (Web site), 56
Cobain, Bev, 123
Colletti-Lafferty, Lorraine, 51
Comaneci, Nadia, 40
Compulsive eating, 36, 37
Contract with self, project, 81
Control, gaining
　　alternative paths, planning positive, 85–90
　　getting things done, 78–83
　　real you, 90–92
　　reasonable standard setting, 84–85
Cooke, Kaz, 15
Cooking, 101
Cousins, Norman, 62
Covey, Sean, 92
Cresswell, Helen, 104
Criticism, 44–47
Crunchy foods, to stay awake, 35
Cruz, Sor Juana Inés de la, 17
Curie, Marie, 17
Cutting, 41–42

D

Daedalus, 22
Dancing on My Grave (Kirkland), 40, 42
Danziger, Paula, 102
Dating, 47–51
Death, 37, 118–122
Delisle, Jim, 4, 114
Depression, 27
Deuker, Carl, 104
DeVito, Danny, 88
Diana, Princess, 41
Dickinson, Emily, 57
Disney, Walt, 58
Do It Now! Break the Procrastination Habit
    (Knaus and Edgerly), 29
Dole, Elizabeth, 68
Don't Sweat the Small Stuff. . . and It's All Small
    Stuff (Carlson), 67
Don't Sweat the Small Stuff with your Family
    (Carlson), 56
Drugs & Your Brain (Grabish), 42
Duda, Joan L., 38–39
Duncan, Isadora, 57

E

Eating disorders, 36–41
Eating Disorders & Food Addiction Resources
    (Web site), 43
Edgerly, John W., 29
Edison, Thomas, 88
Einstein, Albert, 75
Electrolyte imbalance, 37
Elkind, David, 15
Erikson, Erik, 12
Erlbach, Arlene, 67
Espeland, Pamela, 56, 77
Excellence, pursuit of vs. perfectionism, 6, 18
Exercise, 34, 62, 64–65, 101
Expectations and achievements, 9–11

F

Failure, 23–25, 60–61, 122–123
Families, 5, 31, 53
    See also Parents
Favazza, Armando, 41
Feeling Good: The New Mood Therapy (Burns), 114
Females. *See* Gender differences
Feminism, 70–71
Ferrari, Joseph R., 23–25
Fighting Invisible Tigers: A Stress Management
    Guide for Teens (Hipp), 43
Firstborn children, 8–9
Fisher, Carrie, 57
Flexibility, 88, 122–123

Focus, project topic, 79
Fonda, Jane, 40
Food. *See* Eating disorders
Food Fight (Bode), 43
Foods, to stay awake, 35
Ford, Henry, 59
Franz, Dennis, 88
Freeman, Louis, 58
Friend, perfect, 47–51
Future focus, 19

G

Galbraith, Judy, 4, 56, 114
Gates, Bill, 57
Gender differences
    eating disorders, 37
    expectations, 68–69
    perfectionism vs. self-concept, 16
    suicide, 118–119
    Superboy to Superman, 73–75
    Supergirl to Superwoman, 69–73
    woman's movement, 70–71
Geobond, 86
Gershwin, George, 57
Gifted kids, 4
The Gifted Kids Survival Guide (A Teen Handook)
    (Galbraith and Delisle), 4, 114
Giovanni, Nikki, 87
Girl Scouts of the U.S.A., (Web site), 56
Go Tell It On the Mountain (Baldwin), 88
Goal priorities, 20
Going public about perfectionism, 112–114
Gone with the Wind (Mitchell), 29
Goodyear, Charles, 58
Google search engine, 80
Gordon, Sol, 123
Grabish, Beatrice R., 42
Gymnastics, 38–39

H

Hanks, Tom, 88
Harding, Tonya, 5
Henrich, Christy, 38
Hepburn, Katharine, 17
Here's to You, Rachel Robinson (Blume), 103
Hipp, Earl, 42
Hitler, Adolf, 116
Hobbies and play, balance in life, 5
Hoffius, Stephen, 104
Holmes, Oliver Wendell, Jr., 116
How to Get Control of Your Time and Your life
    (Lakein), 92
Hughes, Langston, 88

About the Authors

Miriam Adderholdt, Ph.D., is the AIG (Academically or Intellectually Gifted) teacher at Millingport Elementary School in Stanly County, North Carolina. She received her doctorate in educational psychology from the University of Georgia, Athens, and this book grew out of her dissertation. Miriam has also taught gifted students in grades K–9.

Jan Goldberg is a professional writer and credentialed teacher from Glenview, Illinois. She has authored twenty-six books and more than three hundred articles on education and career development. The mother of three daughters with varying degrees of perfectionism, Jan also conducts writing workshops for aspiring teen authors.